Our Hope Has Come

CELEBRATING THE PROMISE OF **ADVENT**

LIFEWAY WOMEN

Lifeway Press®
Nashville, Tennessee

Published by Lifeway Press® • © 2021 Lifeway Christian Resources •
Nashville, TN

ISBN: 978-1-0877-4786-6
Item: 005833150
Dewey decimal classification: 232
Subject headings: JESUS CHRIST / HOPE / WOMEN

To order additional copies of this resource, write to Lifeway
Resources Customer Service; One Lifeway Plaza; Nashville, TN
37234; order online at www.lifeway.com; fax 615.251.5933;
phone toll free 800.458.2772; or email orderentry@lifeway.com.

Printed in the United States of America

Lifeway Women Publishing • Lifeway Resources •
One Lifeway Plaza • Nashville, TN 37234

EDITORIAL TEAM, LIFEWAY WOMEN BIBLE STUDIES

Becky Loyd
Director, Lifeway Women

Tina Boesch
Manager, Lifeway
Women Bible Studies

Sarah Doss
Editorial Project
Leader, Lifeway
Women Bible Studies

Laura Magness
Content Editor

Lindsey Bush
Production Editor

Lauren Ervin
Graphic Designer

Contents

How to Use This Study

Welcome! We are excited you have chosen to join us as we journey through the Advent season together.

Since many Bible study groups don't meet during this busy season, we've created a study you can do alone, with family, or with friends. In each week's session you'll find:

- An introduction;
- Five days of personal study;
- Activities to do individually (or with your friends and family);
- Activities to do with kids and teens; and
- Group discussion questions.

This study is designed to encourage you and renew your hope in Jesus this Christmas. Use the five days of personal study to reflect, allowing God's Word to challenge you and nourish your soul.

GROUP DISCUSSION

If you decide to do this study with others, use the Group Guide discussion questions found at the start of each week to guide your conversation. In addition to answering the questions in the Group Guide, invite women to share the things they learned from each day of study and verbalize how each week's Scriptures impacted them.

Invite women to tell how they've incorporated the kids, teens, and adult activities into the season of Advent. If you choose, your group may want to bring the supplies needed for completing one of the activities in a group setting as you discuss the Group Guide questions and personal study.

Because Christmastime is inevitably busy, we hope the activities in the study provide a time of rest and reflection. Enjoy sharing the love and hope of Jesus with your family, friends, and neighbors this season.

A GROUP TIME MIGHT LOOK SOMETHING LIKE THIS:

- Welcome. Use this time to light a candle if you choose to incorporate an Advent wreath into your devotional time each week. (Refer to "The Advent Wreath" on pages 156–157 for a detailed guide.)

- Ask the questions on the Group Guide page for that week.

- Review the five days of personal study.

- Ask women to share any special activities they added to their week as they focused on Advent.

- Read Scripture related to the week's theme. You may consider reading a selection of verses from the daily readings or those highlighted in "The Advent Wreath" activity at the back of the book.

- Close in prayer.

SHARE WITH OTHERS

You probably have neighbors who do not understand Advent. Consider inviting others to join you, using the Group Guide questions and hosting a group in your home. Explain the Advent wreath, what the Bible says about Jesus, and how your celebration of the Christmas season is different because of the hope you have in Christ.

Introduction

by Sarah Doss

Don't get your hopes up. Maybe someone offered you that warning recently. Undoubtedly, you've whispered it to yourself before. I know I have many times. Trying not to get our hopes up is an attempt at managing expectations, a well-intentioned effort to protect our hearts from pain or hurt because we know that this world brings its fair share of disappointment and uncertainty. Hope is risky. Maybe if we don't put our hearts into it, we think, we'll be able to bounce back if things don't pan out the way we wish they had. Unmet expectations won't matter as much, or they won't leave quite such a deep cavern of despair.

Sure, there may be times when a refusal to hope is healthy, times when it keeps us grounded in reality. But there are other times when that most certainly is not true. Ecclesiastes 3:11 tells us that God "has put eternity into man's heart" (ESV). In other words, God has placed in us an innate understanding that this life here on earth isn't all there is, that we were made for more. So, when we counsel our hearts not to get their hopes up about things like a better future, freedom from sin, or redemption in relationships, we are pushing up against the reality that the hope of a restored world and eternal life with God lives in our hearts as His children.

Consider the apostle Paul's words in Romans 8:

> For we know that the whole creation has been groaning together with labor pains until now. Not only that, but we ourselves who have the Spirit as the firstfruits—we also groan within ourselves, eagerly waiting for adoption, the redemption of our bodies. Now in this hope we were saved, but hope that is seen is not hope, because who hopes for what he sees? Now if we hope for what we do not see, we eagerly wait for it with patience.
>
> Romans 8:22–25

"In this hope we were saved," the hope of redemption. The hope of God setting everything right and making everything new again begins with the birth of Jesus, God's Son, who came to earth as a baby clothed in full humanity, lived a sinless life, died for us on the cross, and then came back to life again. Also rooted in Jesus is our hope that until He returns, the seed of redemption that has made our stony hearts tender to God will continue to grow, breathing new life into our hearts and minds and souls.

This is Advent—a celebration of the in-between, where we reflect on Jesus' birth and everything it meant for us and our world, while we also hope with eager anticipation for His return. What better way to remind ourselves of the hope we have in Jesus than to celebrate His coming to this earth as a newborn babe, and His coming again as our conquering King.

When Jesus is the sole object of our affections, we have the hope we need to face every mountain top view and valley low voyage we encounter in this life. Hope for peace with God. Hope for identity—the ability to cease striving for the approval of others and rest in who God has made each of us to be. Hope for belonging—a place for the lonely in the family of God. Hope for joy—eternal joy found only in the loving embrace of our heavenly Father.

In our study together, we're going to trace the triumph of hope that was the result of the coming of Christ to this earth. We will see how Jesus fulfilled so many hopes that God had revealed centuries before, how God placed hope in the hearts of His followers in their obedience to His call on their lives, and how the biblical examples of hope deferred can encourage those of us who may be struggling to wait with patience, as Romans 8 so eloquently puts it.

Many of us come to this Bible study in the midst of hard seasons. During those times, "hope talk" can feel like mere lip service, rubbing salt in an open wound, or reminding us of all our unanswered prayers. Even when we know hope is "the right answer," it can be hard to feel it in our hearts.

Dear friend, no matter where you find yourself, God has hope for you. He wants you to bring everything from your wounds to your longings to your dreams and your bursting-at-the-seams joys to Him. He is gentle and kind. He can be trusted, even with a fragile hope. God's Word shows us that He meets our shaky hopes with the unshakable and unchanging reality of who He is. Real hope doesn't let us down because it's fixated on who God is, who He's always been, and who He will always be—our Creator and Redeemer.

We can face the uncertainties of the future with defiant joy in God and the confidence that "hope does not put us to shame, because God's love has been poured into our hearts through the Holy Spirit who has been given to us" (Rom. 5:5). We can rejoice in what God has in store because He loves us, He's a good Father to us, and He's not letting us go.

Whether you've trusted in Jesus for a long time, you find yourself wondering who He is, or you're anywhere in-between, we're so glad you're here. Maybe it's a good time we all get our hopes up after all?

God sent forth His Son

When the fullness of
the time came, God sent
His Son, born of a woman,
born under the Law, so
that He might redeem
those who were under
the Law, that we might
receive the adoption as
sons *and daughters.*
GALATIANS 4:4-5, NASB

Hope
Revealed

THE FATHER'S PROMISE

by Sarah Doss

Hope can be an elusive concept, one that is hard to put into words or may mean different things to different people. The dictionary defines *hope* as "a feeling of expectation and desire for a certain thing to happen; a person or thing that may help or save someone."[1] When I say I'm hoping for something, I'm usually trying to describe the idea of *joyful expectation*— a longing or anticipation of things to come.

As the people of God, Advent is a time of joyful expectation. During Advent we celebrate with joy God's faithfulness to us, seen most clearly in the arrival (or "advent") of Jesus, the fulfillment of so many promises God made to Old Testament saints and His followers today alike. We also look forward with much expectation and hope at Jesus' return, a promise God has yet to fulfill.

The Advent season also serves as a beacon of light in a dark and weary world for people who aren't in the family of God. Even those who wouldn't call themselves followers of Christ stand in the glow of the Christmas season. To quote the classic holiday movie *Home Alone,* "This is Christmas. The season of perpetual hope."[2]

We get to celebrate Jesus' birth knowing the full story of His time on earth, death, and resurrection. But the Bible tells us about brothers and sisters who lived in joyful expectation of Jesus' birth long before it was clear how or when He would come, or what He would accomplish when He did. This week, through snapshots from the lives of Abraham, Jacob, Ruth, David, and Zerubbabel, we'll see our Old Testament faith family members walk steadily down the paths God mapped for them, trusting Him to make their way plain and illuminate each step, though their destinations were unclear. We'll read about how they faced seemingly insurmountable obstacles in their assignments from God and persevered. We'll also trace the hope of Jesus' coming (and what that would mean for God's people) that was revealed in each of their lives.

Their steps of obedience, even in seasons of waiting and sorrow, had far-reaching ramifications to push forward the kingdom of God. And the same is true for our obedience.

These passages have a lot to teach us about faith-filled hope in God's character and what it looks like to trust God's guidance and gifts along the unique path He's picked for each of us. Like the people we will spend time with this week, you'll likely never know on this side of heaven all the ways God will use your life to make His kingdom come on this earth, but He promises to use your steps of faithful obedience for your good and His glory.

These stories also show us what it looks like to rejoice in God's complete and sovereign knowledge and our limited vision. Many of us believe that God is for us, but when our experiences are tough and life doesn't look as we'd planned, it can be easy to abandon our devotion to God and instead put our hope in the temporary relief this world offers.

> In the Advent season, we celebrate God's kindness to us, even as we wait on the future hope of His return.

Thankfully, God is kind toward us in His plans for our individual lives and His plans for the world. In His sovereignty, He works and acts at just the right time as we see clearly modeled in Jesus' birth story. Galatians 4:4 says, "When the fullness of time had come, God sent forth his Son . . ." (ESV). Jesus was born into the world after an incredibly long season of silence from God, the approximately four hundred years of time that elapsed between the Old Testament prophet Malachi and the opening of the New Testament. Even though the people of God couldn't see it, God was working to orchestrate the coming of Christ at just the right time.

We also see God's perfect timing in Jesus' death and resurrection—His rescue of us eternally. Romans 5:6 reminds us, "For while we were still helpless, at the right time, Christ died for the ungodly." That's us, you and me. When Jesus died on the cross, His death was for us and our sins. In the Advent season, we celebrate God's kindness to us, even as we wait on the future hope of His return.

In the end, it seems, hope is more than an expectation. Hope is a trust—trust in God, whose character won't disappoint us if we'll keep traversing this life hand in hand with Him.

1 | In the introduction, *hope* is defined as "joyful expectation." Write your own definition of *hope* in the space provided.

2 | Our ability to hope in God is because of who He has revealed Himself to be in His Word. Make a list of the character traits of God from Scripture that prove He is worthy of your trust and hope. (If you need some help getting started, read Ps. 145.)

3 | Read Galatians 4:4-5. What is the good news of these verses? How can the truth of these verses inform the way you wait and hope today?

4 | In this week's daily readings, we will learn about maintaining hope through obedience, sin struggles, brokenness, long seasons of waiting, and wrenches in our plans. Which of these most resonates with where you find yourself today, and why?

5 | What is something you are hoping God will do in your life or teach you this Advent season? Take some time to pray over that specific hope and surrender it to the Lord.

NOTES

TRUST IN GOD'S PLANS

by Joy Allmond

I come from a long line of late spiritual bloomers. My parents and grandparents all came to Christ as adults. Each night, my great-grandfather Hayes prayed over his seven children—the youngest of whom was my paternal grandfather. One of those consistent prayers was for their salvation. From what I have been told, the thing Hayes cared about most in his life was that his family would be an unbroken one in heaven. By the time my great-grandfather died, none of his children were Christians. But one by one, all seven came to Christ. Although his prayers did not come to fruition while he lived on earth, he never ceased praying, and they were indeed answered.

I'm humbled every time I think about my great-grandfather. I'm humbled because those prayers prayed one hundred years ago covered me, as well. According to the story, he didn't just pray for his kids; he also prayed for his kids' kids. And their kids. And so on.

In some ways, Hayes reminds me of Abraham. Like Abraham, my great-grandfather was obedient to trust and pray as he waited for God to move in a big way. They both hoped for things they could not see (Heb. 11:1), and they both lived faithful lives without seeing the fruit of their obedience. God used the faithfulness of both men to make His name known.

READ GENESIS 12:1-3.

We are introduced to Abraham (initially named Abram) in Genesis 11, where we learn he was a descendant of Noah from Noah's son, Shem. At the start of Genesis 12, we read that God interrupted Abraham's life much like He did Noah's. For Abraham, obedience to God's call was costly. The Lord told him to leave everything he knew, to leave the community that raised him, to leave what he held dear. But Abraham trusted that God's purpose in telling him to make this major life pivot was to accomplish something infinitely greater than anything that involved his comfort.

How do you imagine you would have reacted if you were in Abraham's position?

Reflect on a time when you believed God was calling you to make a sacrifice or do something uncomfortable out of obedience. What seemed hard—or maybe even irrational or counterintuitive—about it? What was the outcome of that step of faith? If you're still waiting to see the outcome, what are you praying while you wait?

Make a list contrasting the promises God made to Abraham in verses 2–3. What stands out to you as you compare your list?

In verse 3, God indicated there would be trouble. He made several "good" promises: He would make Abraham "a great nation"; Abraham would be blessed (and would be "a blessing"); and Abraham's name would be great. But when God promised He would defend Abraham against those who mistreated him, He indicated that the road to seeing faithful obedience rewarded and promises fulfilled wouldn't be easy. In most of our contexts, we aren't suffering outright persecution for obedience. But a life of submission to the Lord and His Word is not free from suffering and hardships.

Describe some ways you have suffered or experienced negative consequences as you waited in obedience to God.

As it turns out, packing up and going to an unknown place with an uncertain future was just the beginning of Abraham's obedience.

READ GENESIS 22:1-19. **What did God tell Abraham to do this time?**

It's hard to imagine being asked to do anything more difficult than what God asked of Abraham in this scene. What does Abraham's obedience here teach us about his relationship with God?

Abraham had seen evidence of God's faithfulness and goodness over many years—through his obedience to leave the land and people he knew and live as a foreigner in a strange place, through the improbable conception of his children, and through God's consistent presence with him. God had shown Himself trustworthy throughout the life of Abraham, and it seems that is what Abraham fixed his eyes on in this very difficult moment.

READ HEBREWS 11:7-11. **List each of the people mentioned and how God worked in their lives.**

What's the common denominator in all of their stories?

The people listed in Hebrews 11:7-11 listened to God and trusted Him to fulfill His promises. Because of their faith in God, they trusted Him to carry them through their circumstances, even when the road ahead was unclear. As a result, God used their obedience and faith to build His kingdom.

> **READ HEBREWS 11:9,13, AND 16.** Summarize these verses in your own words. How does the hope of eternity impact your faith today?

When we're asked to trust and obey, especially in the hard things, it's helpful to remember that this place where we physically dwell isn't our home. The writer of Hebrews reminds us that our ultimate home is in eternity with God. While this world will be wrought with struggles, an enduring faith is worth it because of what is coming—eternity with a loving God, in His holy city, alongside our Immanuel.

> What's God asking of you this Advent season? Is He telling you to do hard things? Is He calling you to sacrifice something important for the sake of your personal holiness or for the spiritual benefit of another person? Spend a few minutes with Him in prayer, confessing what feels hard and renewing your commitment of faith to Him.

Ultimately, every act of obedience we make through faithfulness is for God's glory—not for our personal gain, comfort, or earthly reward. As we wait for Him to work through our circumstances, let's remember that this place where we live and these bodies we have are only temporary. Our purpose for now is to love Him and do what He commands. May God's work through our obedience point to the kingdom that is to come.

TRUST THROUGH YOUR STRUGGLES

by Rachel Shaver

Our jumping off point for today's study is Jesus' genealogy in Matthew. If you're thinking, *The genealogies aren't my favorite part!*, then bear with me. Understanding what God has been doing *for* His people *through* His people since the beginning of time gives us all reason to have solid hope, no matter what our lives look like today. God always does what He says He is going to do, and He can use anyone to accomplish His plans.

READ MATTHEW 1:1-16.

The genealogy of Jesus that Matthew chose for his Gospel begins with Abraham. Abraham fathered Isaac, and Isaac fathered Jacob (v. 2). For today, we'll stop with Jacob, but you'll see several people from this list in the coming days' readings.

Skim Genesis 25–33, and list some of the things you learn about Jacob.

Jacob was chosen by God to play an important role among His people, but Scripture makes it clear that Jacob was far from perfect. He tricked his older twin brother (Esau) out of his birthright (Gen. 25). He fell in love with a girl (Rachel) but was tricked into marrying her sister (Leah) before eventually marrying Rachel, too (Gen. 29). Jacob fathered twelve sons with his wives *and their servants*. Jacob literally wrestled with God (Gen. 32:24-30). Those are just a few notable moments; there's a whole lot more about Jacob that we aren't going to be able to cover today, but suffice it to say, Jacob's history wasn't squeaky clean. He knew the Lord, yes, but the Bible tells us that he was a sinner, just like all of us.

But God.

READ GENESIS 35:1-15.

In Genesis 35, we begin to see a change in Jacob's heart. God told Jacob to go to Bethel, settle there, and build an altar to remember some of the things that God had done for him. In response, Jacob ordered the people with him to get rid of false gods and to purify themselves.

READ GENESIS 35:9-13 AGAIN. What new name did God give Jacob, and what was its significance?

Many times in Scripture we read about God changing a person's name, and it's always for a specific purpose. In this case, God reminded Jacob that He chose him and was working in and through him despite Jacob's past sins and family dysfunction. And the name, *Israel*? In Scripture, it signifies God's chosen people. That's a significant name change.

READ GENESIS 49:10.

While on his deathbed, Jacob gathered his sons to tell them what would happen in the coming days. In verse 10, he told his son, Judah, "The scepter shall not depart from Judah, nor the ruler's staff from between his feet, until tribute comes to him; and to him shall be the obedience of the peoples" (ESV). The scepter indicates royalty and authority, and most scholars agree that "he whose right it is" refers to Jesus.[3] Jesus, the Savior of the world, was to come from the house of Jacob, from the line of Judah. That's a hefty promise from God.

In the New Testament, we read about the fulfillment of this promise. In Luke 1:26-38, the angel Gabriel appeared to Mary and gave her a message from the Lord:

> He will reign over the house of Jacob forever, and his kingdom will have no end.
>
> Luke 1:33

The eternal King who God promised Jacob He would establish through his descendants was about to be born to Mary. Mary was the wife of Joseph, a descendant of Jacob. Remember that genealogy? "And Jacob fathered Joseph the husband of Mary, who gave birth to Jesus who is called the Messiah" (Matt. 1:16).

God always does what He says He is going to do.

It's easy for us to sit back and judge Jacob for the many ways his sin got the better of him. But I don't think it's by accident that Scripture chronicles his weaknesses. I'm more like Jacob than I would care to admit. No, I don't have more than one husband, but I am impatient with the one I do have. I might not steal my sisters' blessings, but I don't always treat them the way I should. I want to pull my hair out at work. I snap at my kids. Instead of doing things "as unto the Lord," I trudge through my day grumbling about everything that isn't going right.

What about you? How do you relate to Jacob today?

Thank God that our salvation doesn't depend on anything we can or can't do! Instead, our hope and salvation depend on the finished work of Christ. God knows that we aren't able to change our sinful hearts on our own. And because He loves us more than we can imagine, He made a way for us in Jesus—the Savior He promised He would send.

READ 1 PETER 2:9-10. **Reflect on who you are in Christ and what God has done for you.**

Just like God worked through Jacob and gave him a new name, He promises to work in us. Through a lifetime of choosing us, loving us, rebuking us, disciplining us, leading us, and *saving us,* God makes us His own. We can find freedom in knowing that we can't do it by ourselves. Instead, we can surrender our lives to Jesus, the Perfecter of our hope and faith—the One who chooses us. *He* is the One who starts a work in our hearts to know and love Him, who leads us to repentance and a saving grace. And *He* is the One who will present us blameless before the Father one day because of what *He* did for us.

God can use anyone to accomplish His plans. How is He using you?

What hope! What relief! Let praise be on our lips this Advent season as we reflect upon God's fulfillment of His promise to Jacob and to each of us: Jesus Christ, our great hope, has come, and He will reign forever.

TRUST FOR WHEN YOU'RE BROKEN

by Connia Nelson

True confession: I love a sappy romance movie. While most romance movies are predictable, they also tend to be charming and redeeming stories. In real life, however, not every romance begins with joyful moments and glittery lights. Some stories start with a problem, a major challenge, an aching concern, or a personal struggle. Such is the story of Ruth.

LET'S BEGIN BY TAKING SOME TIME TO READ OR SKIM RUTH 1–4.

When the Book of Ruth opens, there is a famine in Israel. Because of the famine, Elimelech moved his wife, Naomi, and their two sons, Mahlon and Chilion, to Moab. Ironically, in their attempt to escape suffering of a famine, this family faced immeasurable loss in Moab. Elimelech died, leaving behind Naomi and their sons. Both sons married Moabite women, but within ten years the sons died as well. Naomi's grieving heart must have been utterly broken.

It's hard to imagine the hopelessness Naomi likely felt at the realization that she was destitute. She believed the Lord had turned His hand against her and dealt with her bitterly (Ruth 1:13,20). With overwhelming disappointment, Naomi decided to go home to Bethlehem, and she urged her daughters-in-law to return to their childhood homes. With tears of sadness, Orpah turned back to her home, but Ruth was determined to stay with Naomi. She vowed to go wherever Naomi went and to be committed to Naomi's God and her people (1:16). As Naomi arrived in Bethlehem with Ruth by her side, she returned with nothing but emptiness. However, chapter 1 ends with a glimmer of hope as the barley harvest was about to begin.

> **Like Ruth, you may be facing a difficult decision today or know one is looming in the near future. If so, what do you sense God urging you to do?**

Boaz was a wealthy farmer, a man of noble character, and the son of Rahab. (Yes, the same Rahab who hid the spies during the collapse of Jericho. See Josh. 2 and Matt. 1:5.) During harvest, the Law of Moses commanded the Israelites to leave grain behind for the poor. So, Ruth asked Naomi if she could go to the fields to gather grain, and Naomi agreed. As God would have it, Ruth gathered grain from a field that belonged to Boaz, a man who happened to be a relative of Elimelech.

Ruth's devotion to Naomi and obedience to God's law didn't go unnoticed by Boaz. Boaz was so impressed by Ruth's loyalty to Naomi that he prayed for God to reward her boldness (Ruth 2:11-12). Boaz recognized Ruth as a woman with "noble character" (3:11; also the same words used to describe the woman in Prov. 31). Boaz told his men to pull out stalks from the bundles (the good stuff) for her to gather, not just the fallen scraps. Even though she was a Moabite and not a Jew, Boaz showed her favor. He made sure she was protected in his field and that her food provisions were plentiful (Ruth 2:5-9).

Consider a specific time when you know the favor of God was shown to you by the actions of someone else. How did you feel in that moment?

READ DEUTERONOMY 25:5-10.

When a man died in those days, the custom was for the nearest relative to redeem his land, marry his widow, and have a son on the dead man's behalf. This ensured the man's family name would live on. The relative was known as the kinsman redeemer. Seeing the compassion Boaz had shown Ruth and knowing Boaz was a kinsman redeemer, Naomi suggested to Ruth that she put on her finest perfume and her best dress to offer herself to him as his wife (Ruth 3:3-4). In today's world marriage proposals have become major events with photographers capturing the moment and family members often standing nearby. At Naomi's suggestion, this proposal was privately held at midnight, with Ruth lying down at Boaz's feet and asking him to be her kinsman redeemer (Ruth 3:6-11).

True to form, Boaz immediately told Ruth he wanted to be her kinsman redeemer, but there was a complication. Another family member was a closer relative to Naomi than Boaz. Boaz promised Ruth he would marry her if the other man wasn't able or willing to be her kinsman redeemer. Boaz didn't waste any time in confronting the other relative who was first in line to redeem Naomi's land (3:12–4:1). Initially, the man said he would redeem the land, but when Boaz reminded him that he would have to marry Ruth and have a son in the name of her dead husband, the man refused (4:3-9). So, Boaz became the kinsman redeemer for Ruth and Naomi. He married Ruth, and God gave them a son who was named Obed.

READ MATTHEW 1:1-6. **What does Ruth's inclusion in the family of Jesus tell us about God and the way He works in our world?**

Matthew's genealogy tells us Obed became the grandfather of King David, which means Ruth played a crucial role in the family history of Jesus, the Messiah. Ruth's story began with loss, hardship, and difficult circumstances. Yet the faithfulness, loyalty, and obedience of this Moabite woman were part of God's plan to save the world. Ruth had no idea that as a result of being a poor foreigner gleaning barley in a field, she would find a husband, have a son, become the great-grandmother of King David, and forever be a part of Christ's lineage!

The ultimate love story here isn't about Boaz and Ruth but about the redemptive love of Christ for all humanity and the hope we have in Him. Like Naomi, we are all desperately empty and broken as a result of our sin. Boaz being the kinsman redeemer of both Jew (Naomi) and Gentile (Ruth), gives us a picture of how God loves us all and sent His Son to redeem us from our sins. Jesus Christ is our kinsman redeemer. In Him there is hope eternal.

What comfort and hope does the Book of Ruth offer you today?

If you're honest with yourself, in what or whom do you usually put your hope?

Take a moment to pray and thank God for His redemptive love. Pray by name for people you know who still need to receive this gift of eternal life. Use this season of Advent as a reminder to share the love of Christ with the people in your life who do not yet know Him.

TRUST WHILE YOU WAIT

by Ravin McKelvy

Your presence is my peace.
In the waiting room, you are
the foundation for my trembling
feet. This feat of holding fast to hope,
made possible only by your steady
hand holding me fast. I glory in the
wait, knowing its content and
conclusion are to glorify you.

You may disagree, but I find it much easier to persevere through waiting when I know what's coming. I can work joyfully, knowing I'm going on vacation in a few weeks. I can push through my workout, knowing I'm going to treat myself to French fries later. (Balance is key, right?) But what about when we don't know what's going to happen? The majority of our waiting comes with an unknown end date, and an unknown path to that end. What does it look like to hope while we wait?

READ PSALM 27.

David gives us a wonderful example of how to maintain hope and glorify God through seasons of waiting. When David was anointed king as a young shepherd, he didn't know the road that lay ahead. Instead of an instant crown and authority, he found himself entering what would turn out to be a fifteen-year season of waiting. This was by no means an easy period of time either. David was hunted down by the current king, Saul, he was often alone and in hiding, and he fought in many battles. I'm sure this wasn't what he imagined when he found out he would become king, yet there he was. In the midst of adversity and waiting, David fixed his eyes on the truth of who God is. This didn't change the circumstances of David's waiting, but it did change how he waited.

Read the verses below and record what each one teaches us about how we should wait.

PSALM 37:7

ROMANS 8:19,25

JAMES 5:7-8

We all go through seasons of waiting in our lives. But the most important thing is not what we're waiting on; it's *how* we wait. Believers in Christ are called to hope. Not only are we called to hope, but we've been offered an intimate relationship with the God in whom our hope lies. In seasons of waiting, especially in difficulty, we have a hope that goes beyond our circumstances. Just like we see in the last two verses of Psalm 27, there is an aspect of eager expectation to see the Lord's goodness in the midst of waiting. We are able to wait with strength and courage because of the God in whom we hope.

Are you in a season of waiting? What are you waiting for?

What does it look like to hope in the Lord while you wait?

I know for many of us, even as we cling to hope our times of waiting can still be marked with deep longing. Longing is a feeling common to all of us. It is a felt reminder of a spiritual reality—we are all longing for Christ, for His return, for unhindered communion with Him, and for Him to right everything wrong in our world. Just as all the world was longing for the coming of the Messiah in David's time, all the world is longing for the return of Christ now. So, whether our desires are fulfilled as Psalm 27:13 says, "in the land of the living," or not, we can wait with hope-filled certainty knowing they will be at the return of Christ. Though life may be filled with anguish, we can also see our longing as beautiful because it points us to the certainty of what's to come.

What longings do you have in this season? How do you see those longings pointing you toward Christ?

READ 2 SAMUEL 7.

In 2 Samuel 7, we meet David in a new circumstance. His long season of trial-filled waiting was over, and he was finally king over Israel. Yet, we see here that the end of David's waiting wasn't the end of the story. As David sat in his new palace ("house of cedar," v. 2), his desire was to build a temple for the ark of God. David wanted to glorify God for all He had done both in David's season of waiting and in the fulfillment of His promise.

In his new circumstances, David continued to make much of God. He didn't pull himself up by his bootstraps in the face of adversity or come to be king on his own. It was through the faithfulness of God as he waited that he came to see the prophecy fulfilled. And once king, David didn't abandon God in pursuit of his own glory. We see in his prayer of thanksgiving that David acknowledged how far God had brought him (2 Sam. 7:18-29). Though he didn't do it perfectly, David's reign was a time in which God was glorified in Israel.

We may be tempted to think that the ultimate destination is for our longing to be fulfilled, or our season of waiting to come to an end. But the true end goal of everything is to bring glory to God. Today, as you reflect on the season of waiting you find yourself in, remember to use every moment given you to glorify God.

Write down some specific ways you can use this season of waiting or fulfillment to bring glory to God.

TRUST THROUGH THE UNEXPECTED

by Mary Wiley

We can all agree that life rarely goes how we expect it to go. Oftentimes, the five-year plans we set in place go off course before we make it through the first year (or even first month). An unexpected health diagnosis, job loss, move, loss of a loved one, and on and on can change the trajectories we assume our lives are taking. This is nothing new. Our study today centers on Zerubbabel, an Old Testament figure, and some unexpected challenges the Israelites faced in the time after David ruled the throne.

Think about a time when your life didn't go as planned. How do you remember feeling at the time?

READ HAGGAI 2.

According to this passage, who was Zerubbabel? (Skim Ezra 2–4 to fill in more details.)

A *lot* has happened since David ruled a unified kingdom many generations ago. Zerubbabel was the governor of Judah, a descendant of David, and the grandson of King Jehoiachin (1 Chron. 3:17). David ruled a unified kingdom, but it wasn't long before the north and south began to fight with one another, eventually separating into Israel in the north and Judah in the south. Both of these kingdoms would be conquered and God's people exiled. Babylon destroyed the temple, along with all of Jerusalem's walls (2 Chron. 36:19). Zerubbabel, heir to the Davidic throne, wasn't born into a palace like we might expect. Instead, he was born in Babylon while God's people were trapped in exile.

This was a season of great suffering and uncertainty for God's people. They had been removed from the land God promised to them and pagan nations ruled over them. God's people had been told the promised Messiah, their great Deliverer, would come from Bethlehem, from Nazareth, and they were far away from there.

Place yourself in the shoes of those who were exiled from Jerusalem. You were God's chosen people, living in His promised land. You were comfortable worshiping at the temple and smelling the burning of incense and offerings, but now life looks completely different. You're forced to leave your home and the promised land to live in a place that is not your own, and the holy temple and your city are destroyed. How would you feel?

God's people longed to return to their land, and seventy years later, God would work in the heart of King Cyrus, moving him to issue a decree allowing God's people to return (Jer. 29:10; Ezra 1:1-4). And who led the charge, bringing more than 42,000 people back to Judah? That's right, Zerubbabel!

God preserved a remnant of His people while they were in exile, and He would provide an opportunity for them to return to the land, re-establishing God's promised Davidic throne. Zerubbabel led well, helping to rebuild the temple and reminding God's people that they weren't forgotten, despite their long season of waiting, disruption, and suffering. God would keep His promise to David to establish His throne forever (2 Sam. 7), and Zerubbabel was a key piece in the puzzle.

REVISIT HAGGAI 2:1-9. **What "house" does this passage reference?**

What's the promise God made about this house in verse 9?

God referred to the temple in Jerusalem as His "house" (v. 3). The people who saw the first temple built by Solomon remembered its glory (1 Kings 6) and mourned the smaller, less impressive temple Zerubbabel and Joshua of Jehozadak were building. Yet, God promised His presence was with them and this smaller temple would outshine the first. How could this be possible?

The promise of this new temple is peace (v. 9), a peace that only God can grant. Peace, a coveted concept for people who lived in exile without any idea of what tomorrow

might look like or when they'd be able to return home. This peace, eternal peace, would come ultimately with Christ, who would be dedicated in this very temple and about whom Simeon would proclaim,

> My eyes have seen your salvation. You have prepared it in the presence of all peoples—a light for revelation to the Gentiles and glory to your people Israel.

Luke 2:30-32

The peace God promised wouldn't come quickly, though. About 500 years spanned the completion of the temple work Zerubbabel led and the coming of Christ. Yet, even half a century before true peace would come, God dwelled with His people through His presence in the temple, and He prepared them for the coming Messiah.

LOOK AGAIN AT HAGGAI 2:10-19. **What did God say about the people and the nation in these verses?**

What actions had God taken against His people and for what purpose? (See v. 17.)

Despite the people's disobedience and inability to stay pure and undefiled before God, He wouldn't walk away from them. Despite their refusal to return to Him even when He used challenging circumstances to highlight their needs and draw them back, He would still bless them from this day forward. This is the kindness of God in our waiting and in our struggles with sin. When we are faithless, He is faithful.

NOW REREAD HAGGAI 2:20-23.

This is a compelling picture of God raising Zerubbabel up as His representative, His signet ring or stamp of authoritative approval. A signet ring had a unique carving that could be pressed into a drop of wax to prove the authenticity of a king's written decree. God would use Zerubbabel as a stamp on His people, working to restore what was lost and continuing to press toward a day when the Messiah would offer restoration and redemption to all.

READ MATTHEW 1:13-16. **How many generations passed between Zerubbabel and Jesus' birth?**

A long season of waiting occurred between the finalization of the temple and the appearance of the angel to Mary and then Joseph. For a while it seemed God was silent, and His people were without guidance. But God kept His promise! All the years of waiting and hoping eventually came to an end, and Immanuel (God with us) entered our world.

Today, we have the blessing of viewing the history of Israel and the coming of Christ in retrospect. The wait is muted to us because we know the rest of the story. Zerubbabel didn't have this blessing, yet he followed God faithfully and did the work asked of him to bring about one of the many steps necessary before God's people would welcome the Messiah.

We no longer look forward to the first coming of a Messiah like Zerubbabel did, because we know He has come. Yet, we do longingly await His return. May we also wait faithfully!

What might it look like for you to wait faithfully now? Write down two or three ways the hope you have in Jesus' return can influence your daily life this Advent season.

NOTES

BIRD FEEDER WREATH

by Lauren Ervin

Whatever your obstacle this Christmas season, cling to the hope that God has not left your story unfinished and unredeemed. He is committed to His people. When you find yourself before an obstacle or in a season of waiting, don't rely on your own strength. Commune with God. Let prayer be your first plan of action, rather than your last resort.

GATHER

- 1 envelope unflavored gelatin
- 1/2 cup hot water
- 3/4 cup flour
- 3 Tbsp. corn syrup
- 4 cups birdseed
- *Bundt pan or mold
- Nonstick spray

*If you want to fill your Bundt pan, you'll need to double the ingredients.

DIRECTIONS

Spray your Bundt pan/mold liberally with nonstick spray. Mix the gelatin packet with hot water until dissolved. Stir in the flour and corn syrup until mixed with the gelatin, then add your birdseed and combine. Pour or scoop your mixture into your pan or mold, pressing down with the back of a spoon. If you're using a wire ring in the middle of your mold, add half your mixture, then the wire, then top the wire with the seed. Place your mold in the refrigerator or somewhere cold to set and firm up. After 24 hours, remove your seed wreath.

Now hang your bird feeder outside. Every time you glance over and see a critter enjoying it this week, pray. Pray for your neighbors, family, and leaders. Pray to have obedience during a season of waiting or courage to face hard things. I hope you feed many birds and bring all your thoughts to the Lord.

TEENS

FOLLOWING IN FAITH

by Karen Daniel

Throughout history, God's people have faced seemingly insurmountable obstacles. Imagine forty years wandering in a desert. Or being under the rule of a king who forces you to worship only his gods. Or how about not hearing a single word from God for hundreds of years?

Even today, as we imagine the future state of our world, I'm sure we've all wondered at times when God will finally step in to "fix" the brokenness. Not having the answers we think we need when we need them can make some circumstances seem hopeless.

Your teens are facing obstacles of their own right now. Big decisions are coming at them every day like a freight train at top speed. And typically the answers don't come easily or quickly.

Take some time this week to read Genesis 12:1-3 together. In verse 1, we see God present Abram with what seems like a huge "ask." He told Abram to leave behind everything he knew, along with all the comforts of home and family, and "go." There were no phones or post offices, so leaving meant leaving. Cutting ties. Moving out. God didn't even specify where, He just vaguely indicated that He'd get to that later. Seem risky? Keep reading.

Of course it seemed risky, but God wouldn't leave Abram on his own. Verses 2-3 are riddled with assurance of God's presence and promises, the greatest of which point to the coming of a Savior for all.

Let's look at the passage again, but this time let's modify it a little and substitute Abram's name with one of your parents' or grandparents' names.

> **The LORD said to**
>
> _____:
>
> **Go. I will bless you, and you will be a blessing. Many people will be blessed because of you.**

Think about someone in your family who was willing to trust God enough to "go" as He instructed. Maybe they didn't have to leave their home or family; they just responded in obedience to what God asked. Abraham's obedience paved the way for God's people. Is it possible your family member's obedience is the reason you celebrate the birth of Christ today? Read it one more time, this time writing in your own name. How will you respond to God's call for obedience?

Know that no matter what obstacles or decisions are barreling down those tracks, hope is real. God has provided a Savior, and His presence and promise will always be with you. And best of all, He won't only bless you—He'll bless others through you.

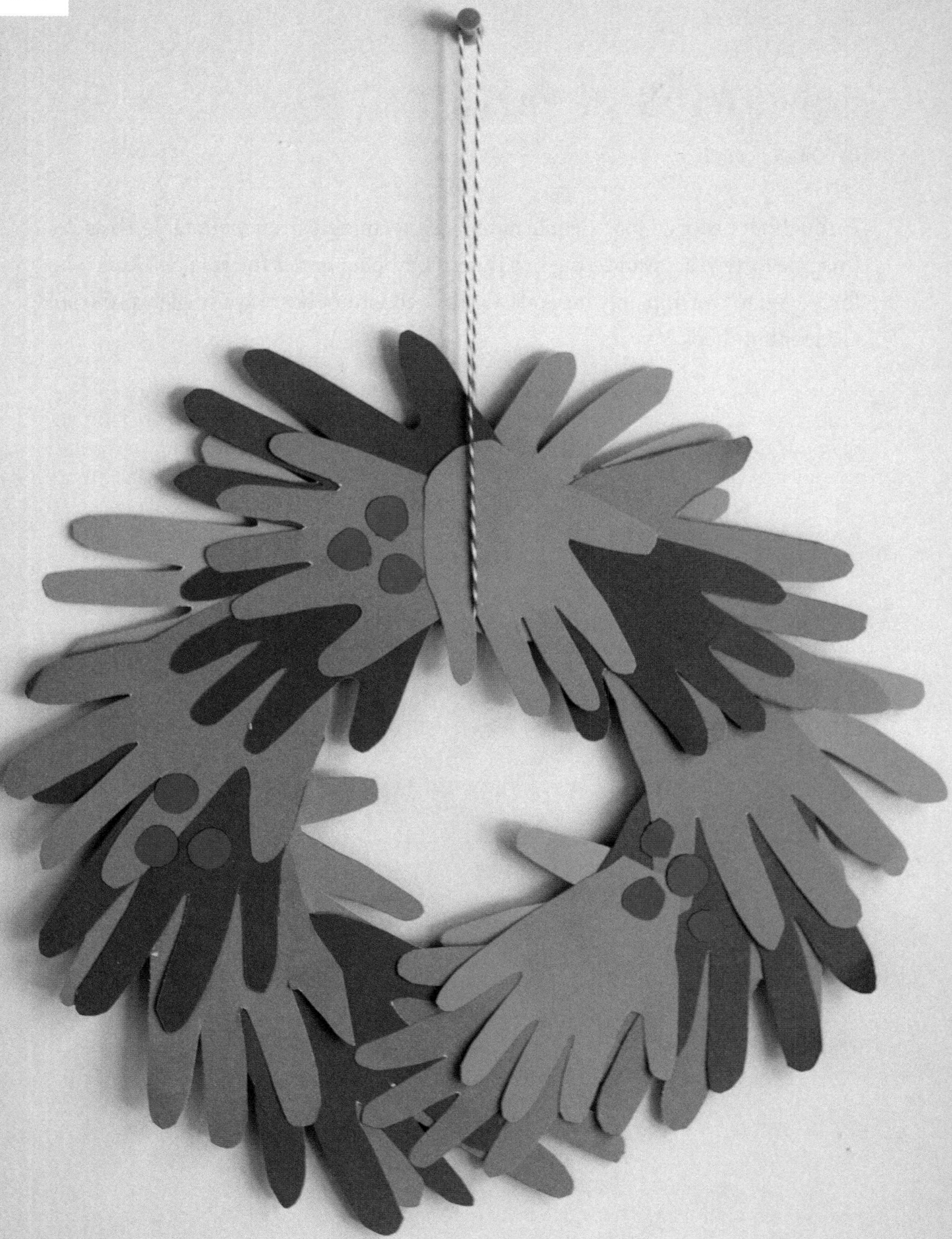

MAKE A FAMILY HANDPRINT WREATH

by Bekah Stoneking

Have you ever stood in a really long line? Or waited a few weeks to celebrate a special day? Waiting for something you're hoping for can be hard, and you might begin to feel impatient. But God doesn't waste time. In His plans, even time spent waiting has a purpose.

GATHER

- Green construction paper
- A paper plate
- Markers
- Scissors
- Liquid glue
- A hole puncher
- Yarn or ribbon

DIRECTIONS

Trace your family members' hands on the construction paper. Cut out at least 10–12 handprints, and cut out the center of the paper plate.

Glue the handprints around the rim of the plate to make a wreath. It works best if you glue the larger handprints first, and then glue a second layer of smaller handprints on top of them.

If you want, add decorations to your wreath, using the hole puncher to make a hole at the top. Tie the yarn or ribbon through the hole. Then find the perfect place to display your family wreath.

GAME

Play "Red Light, Green Light." Have your child stand at a starting line. When you say "green light" the child moves forward toward you, until you say "red light!" Vary the amount of time you stay stopped on red. Ask, *How did you feel while you were stopped and waiting for the fun to start back up?*

In Matthew 1:1-17, forty-two generations are listed. That's hundreds of years between Abraham and Jesus' birth! You stopped and waited for only a few moments during your activity, but God's people watched and waited for a very long time for God to send His promised Messiah. In the meantime, God used many families in His good plan to reveal His faithfulness and to send Jesus to earth at exactly the right time.

PRAY

God, thank You for our family and friends, and thank You for the generations of families You worked through to send Jesus. Thank You for revealing Yourself through the Bible and for showing us that You are faithful, trustworthy, and that You always keep Your promises. Amen.

a child
will
be born
for us

For a child will be born
for us, a son will be given
to us, and the government
will be on his shoulders.
He will be named
Wonderful Counselor,
Mighty God, Eternal
Father, Prince of Peace.
ISAIAH 9:6

Hope
Fulfilled

THE SON'S LOVE

by Sarah Doss

As a child, the movie *The Wizard of Oz* was one of my favorites. I was dazzled by lovely Glenda and the yellow brick road, and in my "musical phase" I butchered more than my fair share of those beloved routines with my imaginary ruby slippers. If you've seen the movie, then (spoiler alert!) you'll remember the scene where the giant floating head "wizard" terrifies Dorothy, until Toto pulls back the curtain to reveal an elderly man controlling all the theatrics.

When I think about this scene, I can't help but compare it to the elementary view of God I've had in the past. For many of us, it's easy to think of God in this puppet master type of way—relationally removed from His creation but controlling it nonetheless. However, this is not the way the Bible describes God.

Throughout the Old Testament, we often see God work through relationships with individual people like the ones we read about last week. And then in the New Testament, Jesus' coming to earth pulled back the curtain for us even further.

The truth is there are aspects of God's character that are incomprehensible for us. God is so hard for us to understand because there's nothing else in all of creation like Him. We need Him to reveal Himself to us and help us understand Him, and thankfully He does just that! God in His grace has chosen to reveal Himself to us, to delight us with glimpses of who He is—which He does through the world around us, His message in Scripture, and the people made in His image—and to make a way for us to have a relationship with Him through Jesus' life and death on the cross.

Much of what we know about God comes from what He revealed about Himself through Jesus, Immanuel, God with us. In His time on earth, Jesus showed us God's character—who He is and how He acts. As we read about Jesus' interactions with people in the New Testament and see how He loved and where His passions lay, we come to know God more, to trust Him more.

In the story of Jesus' coming to earth and the details of His time here, we are also given a model for hope, resilience, and trust amidst seasons of searching and waiting. The prophets of old foretold the coming of a rescuer. And yet, Jesus wasn't who the saints of old expected. They were on the lookout for a powerful, flashy military leader who would lead them to victory and fight their battles.

To be sure, Jesus fought for them (and fights for us), but He fought for their hearts, for their freedom from sin and their undivided worship. Not exactly a savvy political strategy. Let's just say Jesus probably wouldn't have been asked to contribute a chapter to a first-century version of Dale Carnegie's classic business book *How to Win Friends and Influence People*. He has a different definition of success, and He beckons us to follow Him down the narrow path that leads to true life and godliness but disavows so much of what our world holds high.

> God promises joy in abundance when we say yes to His leading, even when we can't quite see the big picture.

This week we're going to focus on some more "traditional" Christmas narratives—the angel's unorthodox birth announcements to Mary and Zechariah, the account of the shepherds and magi coming to worship Jesus, and the long-awaited joy of Simeon and Anna upon meeting the Messiah. In the story of Jesus' birth, God helps us see the fulfillment of the Old Testament prophecies in Jesus, to celebrate the promise of His advent here on earth.

God so often works in ways that feel mysterious to us. After all, He sent a newborn baby, God the Son in flesh, to be the Rescuer for His people. The Bible tells us, "God has chosen what is foolish in the world to shame the wise, and God has chosen what is weak in the world to shame the strong" (1 Cor. 1:27). As we read these biblical accounts of God's faithful children who received unexpected gifts from Him, we pray that your hearts would be encouraged to trust God for good endings to your own stories.

At the same time, we are reminded that God rewards the faithful. Psalm 16:11 says, speaking of God, "You reveal the path of life to me; in your presence is abundant joy; at your right hand are eternal pleasures." In other words, God made us, and He knows the way to lives of peace and flourishing for us. God promises joy in abundance when we say yes to His leading, even when we can't quite see the big picture.

We pray that these passages will encourage your heart to trust God to sustain you along your sojourn here on earth. We also pray these examples of faithfulness will help you stay engaged, present, and steadfastly resilient in your part of the larger redemptive narrative that God began years and years ago and is still weaving together today.

Yes, *you*. God wants to use your life to bring Him glory and point people to Jesus, just like He used Mary's, Elizabeth's, and Anna's. So, whatever you're facing, may the faithfulness of those who have gone before you and the reminders of God's good kindness buoy your soul and help you hold onto hope, even in seasons that feel less hope-filled.

As Zach Eswine said in *Spurgeon's Sorrows*, "Realistic hope is a Jesus-saturated thing."[1] This week, may God re-align our hopes around Jesus, so we can be delighted by the glimpses of God's glory at work in and through us.

1 | The birth of Jesus was surprising in many ways. What are some of the biggest surprises that stand out to you?

2 | Read Luke 1:26-33. What do we learn about Jesus from Gabriel's statement to Mary?

3 | At its heart, Advent is a celebration of Jesus' birth. Why was Jesus' birth the fulfillment of hope for people in the first century? Why is it the fulfillment of your hope, too? Read Ephesians 2:1-10 as you think about this question.

4 | Make a list of the people we meet in the Christmas story. Then spend a few minutes discussing how each person or group of people responded to the news of Jesus' birth (e.g., Mary's joy, Herod's fear, the shepherds' excitement, the wise men's worship, and so on). Which response feels most in line with your relationship with Jesus today, and why?

5 | God used every person and detail from the Christmas story to bring Him glory and point people to Jesus. Spend some time in prayer, asking God to work through each of you in the same way this week.

NOTES

BELIEVE IN GOD'S POWER

by Tina Boesch

Christmas smells like gingerbread and mulled cider to me. When ginger, cinnamon, and cloves mingle, they conjure up decades of memories. They remind me of piping frosting on ginger cookies with my sisters when I was a child. I'm transported back to candlelit walks through the streets of Williamsburg, Virginia, when steaming cider ladled into paper cups warmed my numb hands. And I have a vivid memory of holding my daughter in my lap while reading Scripture before lighting the Advent candles arranged in the middle of our kitchen table.

Just as certain scents can be laden with memory, evoking a larger context, environment, and history, certain phrases in a story can do the same. Allusions to Old Testament passages in the New Testament work this way. A phrase, quote, or reference is meant to call to mind the larger context of the story, inform our understanding, and help us grasp how coherent God's story is from start to finish.

SPEND SOME TIME READING LUKE 1:26-38.

When we read Luke's account of the angel Gabriel's visit to a young woman named Mary, we'll miss a lot of the meaning if we're unaware that the details of the encounter are loaded with references to stories of God's history with His people recorded in the pages of the Old Testament. Growing up in a Jewish community in Nazareth, Mary's identity would have been shaped by the stories she had heard told repeatedly. Her faith in God and her hope that He would ultimately fulfill His promises had been forged by her awareness of God's revelation through His interactions with figures like Abraham, Sarah, and Moses.

When the angel Gabriel appeared to Mary, it's possible she recalled that Gabriel had visited Daniel in Persia while he was serving Belshazzar and later Darius the king of the Chaldeans (Dan. 8:1-26; 9:1,20-23). Gabriel's mission then was to help Daniel understand the visions that God had revealed to him (see Dan. 8:15-17). Gabriel provided insight into realities that Daniel had glimpsed but could not understand. He conveyed God's message and also explained it, just as he did in his conversation with Mary.

The way Mary understood Gabriel's announcement to her—"Greetings, favored woman! The Lord is with you" (Luke 1:28)—would have been shaped by her awareness of God's work in the past. Let's take a moment to look back at some of the stories that this particular greeting may have brought to the mind of someone steeped in the stories of Israel's history.

READ GENESIS 6:8-9. **Who does this passage say was favored by God? How is this man described?**

READ EXODUS 33:12-17. **Who had found favor in God's sight?**

How would it be known that the people had found favor with God? (See Ex. 33:16.)

In the two passages in Genesis and Exodus we just read, God's favor rested on individuals He called to be obedient to difficult tasks. Noah was chosen to rescue his family from the flood of God's judgment by being obedient to build an ark. And Moses was selected to lead God's people from slavery in Egypt to the promised land. Both were favored by God. But God's favor didn't mean they were spared challenging, painful circumstances; it meant God would be with them in the work to which He was calling them. The idea that God was now singling Mary out for a mission must have been daunting. But just wait, there's more . . .

READ JUDGES 6:11-16. **How did the angel of the Lord greet Gideon?**

What did the angel ask Gideon to do? What was Gideon's response?

Gabriel's greeting of Mary echoed the angel's proclamation to Gideon, "The LORD is with you" (Judg. 6:12). Luke reports that Mary was "deeply troubled" by this greeting (Luke 1:29).

> **Given what you've seen in Genesis 6, Exodus 33, and Judges 6, why do you think Mary may have felt deeply troubled when she heard Gabriel's greeting?**

Mary was likely familiar with the full import of being a recipient of God's favor and presence. Jews well acquainted with the Torah (the first five books of the Bible) and Israel's history knew that God's favor rested on figures like Noah, Moses, and Gideon. Gideon was called to save God's people by leading a select army against the Midianites. He was a reluctant but creative warrior who defeated an army of thousands with a few hundred men. In Israel men like these were revered because they were vessels through which God preserved His people.

But what about Mary? Mary was just a young woman from a rural village. She wasn't a builder, a leader, a soldier, or a prophet. But she was a woman who believed the stories she had heard all her life about a God who kept His promises and rescued His people. She knew that He called ordinary people into His service and accomplished things through them that they could never have done in their own strength.

When Mary heard Gabriel's stunning announcement that she was being called to bear a son who would establish an eternal kingdom, inheriting David's throne and reigning "over the house of Jacob forever" (Luke 1:33), she didn't ask if it would happen; she wondered how it could happen through her. Mary, like any faithful Israelite, would have expected a king to come as a fulfillment of the prophetic promises found in passages like 2 Samuel 7:9-16; Isaiah 9:6-7; and Daniel 7:13-14. But Mary almost certainly didn't expect to be so intimately involved in God's rescue plan. The particularity of this call—to mother the Son of God Most High—shattered her expectations.

Under the circumstances, "How can this be?" (Luke 1:34) was a very appropriate question. Mary's query didn't reveal doubt in God's faithfulness; it likely reflected her amazement that He would call her to be a participant in His mission. And it revealed a practical concern: How could a virgin who had never been intimate with a man become a mother? Gabriel's response to Mary alluded to the most famous miraculous birth in the history of Israel: the birth of Isaac to Sarah, a barren, geriatric mother (Gen. 21). The phrase, "For nothing will be impossible with God" (Luke 1:37), evokes Genesis 18:14 and the sharp reminder to Abraham and Sarah that nothing is too hard for God.

Blessed Mary. She said yes to God. Mary's answer, "See, I am the Lord's servant . . . May it happen to me as you have said" (Luke 1:38), is a resounding yes to God's demanding call on her life. Her yes risked her reputation. Many would have assumed that she had been unfaithful to her betrothed husband, Joseph. Her yes risked the discomfort and dangers of pregnancy. She risked social isolation. Still, she said yes!

Mary's yes encompassed more than her agreement to deliver and raise a child. Her yes included her affirmation of all this child was promised to be and accomplish. Her belief marks her as the first disciple of Christ.

Is there a yes that you need to say to God? Explain.

.

How might Mary's faith encourage you today?

Belief is the beginning of a faithful life. The willingness to serve in any capacity assigned by God is the path of discipleship. Mary believed, embracing her calling as a servant of the Lord.

READ ALOUD MARY'S HYMN IN LUKE 1:46-55.

Preparation creates expectation. And expectation fulfilled inspires celebration. God had patiently prepared His people for the arrival of His Son. Mary was ready to welcome the Messiah. She had anticipated His coming. And the fulfillment of her hopes inspired her to celebrate. Her hymn expressed the joy of those who had waited with anticipation that God would mercifully intervene to deliver them from suffering, exile, and oppression.

Her song reflects the culmination of all her hopes. Preparation, expectation, celebration—that's the movement of the Christmas season.

Notice that there's a beautiful balance between the personal and corporate implications of salvation in Mary's hymn. Her song opens with a deeply personal statement,

> My soul magnifies the Lord,
> and my spirit rejoices in God my Savior.

Luke 1:46b–47

Circle the personal pronouns in the lines above. Then look back at the hymn as a whole and note how the personal pronouns in Mary's song change from first person singular in verses 46–49 to third person plural in verses 50–55.

Mary recognized the Lord had done something for her personally: "The Mighty One has done great things *for me*, and his name is holy" (Luke 1:49, emphasis added). That awareness then led her to dwell on the implications of this child's coming for all. She perceived that the promised Son—the holy One, the Mighty God come in the flesh—was not just hers; He was for all people. And the rescue God would orchestrate through Him would be for all who, like Mary, believe and respond with faith.

Today, spend some time delighting in the hymn composed by a woman who believed God. Dwell on the reality that God faithfully keeps His promises. Praise God for the great things He has done in your life this year and anticipate His future coming.

DAY 2

BELIEVE IN GOD'S WISDOM

by Tessa Morrell

I imagine most, if not all, of us have a specific memory of a Christmas as a child when we wanted a particular toy or gift. Every season has an "it" toy, but more than that every child has something special they long for. But who are we kidding? Longings don't go away as we get older, they just change form! From an early age, our desires are strong, and we all have dreams nestled deep in our hearts for both the big and the small things.

Today we're looking at the lives of Elizabeth and Zechariah as they intersect with the Christmas story. These two faithful Jews knew what it felt like to long for something— they had longed for a child for decades. Let's read their story and marvel at the mercy of God as He fulfilled the hopes of this godly couple.

READ LUKE 1:5-7.

What are some of the details we learn about Zechariah and Elizabeth in these first few verses? List them here.

Elizabeth and Zechariah were righteous followers of God. Zechariah was a priest, and Elizabeth was from a family of priests as one of the "daughters of Aaron" (Luke 1:5). They kept God's commands and devoted their lives to Him. Still, they never had children "because Elizabeth could not conceive, and both of them were well along in years" (v. 7). Their days of hoping and praying for a child had long since passed. But that didn't matter to God.

READ LUKE 1:8-17.

The first thing the angel told Zechariah after calming his fears was, "Your prayer has been heard" (v. 13). How many years had Zechariah and Elizabeth prayed for a child? And how many years had it been since they had given up hope of that child ever being a reality in their lives? Regardless, God heard their prayers and knew their hopes.

Have you been praying the same prayer for a long time, perhaps for years or even decades? What helps you not grow weary in continuing that prayer? Or if you are weary, what keeps you praying it anyway?

When our desperate prayers carry over year after year, we may lose hope that God is listening, but the Bible tells us He is. God always hears our prayers (Ps. 145:18-19; Prov. 15:29; 1 John 5:14-15). He cares deeply for us, and He wants to hear what's on our hearts (1 Pet. 5:7).

So often prayer is as much about the work the Lord does in our own hearts as it is about Him answering our prayers. As we keep our eyes fixed on Jesus and steep our hearts in His Word, we discover that the Giver is far greater than the gifts we desire. Even in our deepest aches and most fervent longings, His presence as we pray is a gift in and of itself.

Whether we've been praying for a few days or a few decades, it's important to remember that prayer is about continually talking to the Lord. More than just asking for things, prayer is about developing an ongoing relationship with our heavenly Father, a conversation that helps us grow more in tune with His will for our lives and shapes us into Jesus' image. But that doesn't mean we can't ask for things. In fact, Jesus tells us to do just that: "Ask, and it will be given to you. Seek, and you will find. Knock, and the door will be opened to you" (Matt. 7:7). God wants us to ask Him for what we need or hope for. He hears every word—even every utterance we can't articulate (Rom. 8:26-27)—and He answers all our prayers in accordance with His will.

READ LUKE 1:13-17 AGAIN. **Who would the child be and what would he do? Summarize what the angel told Zechariah about his son.**

This son whose birth defied all reason would have an important role in the life of Jesus, another baby whose birth was unexpected and who came at exactly the right time (Gal. 4:4). John was appointed from before his birth to serve God as a prophet who would encourage people to repent of their sins, return to God, and prepare for the Messiah, God's Promised One. God had a very specific reason for answering Zechariah and Elizabeth's prayer.

READ LUKE 1:18-25.

Why do you think Zechariah doubted what the angel told him?

What tempts you to doubt God's promises?

Zechariah's initial response to the angel was one of doubt and skepticism, which makes sense considering the news he received. Practically speaking, Elizabeth and Zechariah were older people. Their biological window for childbearing had come and gone, and they didn't have any reason to think having a child was still possible. But their time frame wasn't the same as the Lord's. Nothing could stop God from fulfilling His plan and doing the impossible—giving Elizabeth and Zechariah a son. Gabriel told Zechariah that because he doubted what he was told (words Gabriel delivered from God Himself), he wouldn't speak again until the child had been born and named John.

To be honest, there may be times when God's promises feel too good to be true. The world feels too dark. Our circumstances feel too painful. Our hearts feel too broken. And yet, because God's promises are rooted in His character and not in our circumstances, we can trust every single one. Without fail, God keeps every promise. His Word tells us He's true. His Spirit affirms that He's true. When we open our hearts to the possibility that He is trustworthy, He will never, ever let us down. Nothing—not even the "impossible"—will keep God from fulfilling His plans and purposes.

How did Elizabeth respond when she discovered she was pregnant (v. 25)?

Elizabeth's heart praised the One who answered her prayers. She saw God's grace and mercy in this miracle, and she rejoiced in His goodness. Trusting in the Lord isn't always easy when our circumstances are unclear or difficult. However, the Lord brings encouragement and hope for us even on the darkest days through His Word and His presence.

READ LUKE 1:57-80.

For more than nine long months, Zechariah couldn't speak. He was daily reminded of his moment of doubt, but that didn't stop the praise from flowing from his lips the moment he could speak again. The lessons he had learned about God and His faithfulness during this season of silence must have been remarkable. And praise rang forth from the overflow of a heart in awe of God's faithfulness.

What stands out to you from Zechariah's words?

At the end of this eventful first chapter of Luke, the Holy Spirit filled Zechariah, and he proclaimed a prophecy about what God would do through not only his son, but even more importantly through the Messiah who would bring all these things to pass. He spoke of salvation and rescue and forgiveness and peace.

That's the story of Advent and the truth for us to carry through this Christmas season. God's merciful compassion overflowed to humanity through the birth of a baby boy who would "visit us from on high to give light to those who sit in darkness and in the shadow of death, to guide our feet into the way of peace" (vv. 78-79, ESV). God's promises of salvation and peace came true in Jesus, and they continue to come true in our lives today because of Jesus.

The story of Zechariah, Elizabeth, and John is a reminder that often the sweetest answers to prayer are the most unexpected and unlikely. When we've given up hope, that's when God reminds us that He is still working. He is still faithful. And He is the fulfillment of our hope.

What's one way your prayer life can be impacted or encouraged by the story of Zechariah and Elizabeth?

On a sticky note or index card, write a brief prayer of praise to God for His faithful fulfillment of His promises. Keep that prayer with you or hang it somewhere you'll see it often. When you feel discouraged or begin to doubt, come back to that prayer and remind yourself that God is trustworthy and true.

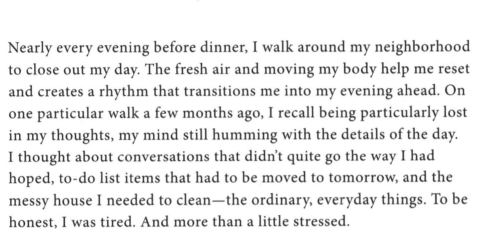

DAY 3

BELIEVE IN GOD'S GOODNESS

by Jessica Yentzer

Nearly every evening before dinner, I walk around my neighborhood to close out my day. The fresh air and moving my body help me reset and creates a rhythm that transitions me into my evening ahead. On one particular walk a few months ago, I recall being particularly lost in my thoughts, my mind still humming with the details of the day. I thought about conversations that didn't quite go the way I had hoped, to-do list items that had to be moved to tomorrow, and the messy house I needed to clean—the ordinary, everyday things. To be honest, I was tired. And more than a little stressed.

As the day slowly faded into evening and I neared the end of my walk, I felt the sudden urge to turn around. When I did, I was met by the most beautiful sunset. There I was—in the middle of the road—stunned. I smiled and exhaled slowly, feeling myself relax. What a gift to be reminded that the God who crafted that sunset also crafts my days. I love that our extraordinary God chases us into our ordinary moments if for no other reason than to remind us of who He is and who we are in Him.

Today's passage from the Christmas story is a familiar one, but that shouldn't make it any less impactful. This scene gives us great insight into how God works in our world—the extraordinary divine intersected with the lives of ordinary shepherds in an ordinary moment on an ordinary hillside.

READ LUKE 2:8-20.

Many of us have read or heard this passage so many times that we've stopped being stunned by the wonder of what the shepherds saw that night. Take a moment to pray that the Lord would help you see this familiar story in a fresh way. Then, read Luke 2:8-20 one more time, visualizing the scene and letting the words sink in.

The shepherds were an interesting, even surprising, choice to receive the news of the Messiah's birth. Rather than the angels appearing to a group of Jewish religious leaders at the temple like we might expect, God chose to share the news with a group of men who held a messy, even despised occupation and spent their days isolated from the rest of their community.[2] This is good news for ordinary people like us, and it sets the stage for all the ways Jesus' life and ministry defied expectations.

> **What are some reasons you are encouraged that the angel of the Lord visited ordinary shepherds?**

> **READ LUKE 2:11. Who did the angel of the Lord say the Savior was born for?**

Did you catch that? The angel of the Lord delivered this good news that the Savior had been born *for these shepherds* ("for you")! Not only did they get to hear the news first, but they would be recipients of this Savior's life-saving work, just like Mary, Elizabeth, and Zechariah were. And just like you and I are, too.

After the first angel's announcement, a whole chorus of angels appeared in a moment that puts my sunset walk to shame. We don't know exactly how long this experience between the angels and the shepherds lasted, but we can tell from the shepherds' response that it was spectacular. At first, they were terrified. But after the angel's words not to be afraid and the good news that followed, we see the shepherds respond with excitement.

> **READ LUKE 2:15. Note what the shepherds did after the angels left. What strikes you most about the shepherds' response to the good news?**

Both the haste and the faith with which the shepherds responded to the angels is impressive. The shepherds didn't delay in going to find the baby in the manger. They didn't ask questions, they didn't make plans to go find the baby "tomorrow," and they didn't seem to find someone to watch the sheep. Nothing slowed them down from seeing this promise fulfilled.

The shepherds' faith is also remarkable—they believed the angel and did as they were told. Although it would seem foolish for them to respond with doubt in the face of such a stunning proclamation from the angels, how many times do we respond to evidence of God's work with doubt? How many times do we forget that the fulfillment of our hope is just as certain as the shepherds' was that night? Our hope today is fixed on that very same baby born in Bethlehem, which means the shepherds' good news of a Savior is good news for us, too.

What are some things that cause you to doubt the certain hope you have in Christ?

Read the verses below and record the truths you learn about your hope in Christ.

HEBREWS 6:19

ROMANS 15:12-13

1 PETER 1:3

Whenever I find myself paralyzed by doubts and questions instead of stepping forward in faith, I know that my perspective needs to be shifted. Don't get me wrong—asking good questions can be a healthy thing, but sometimes we need to take steps of faith without having all the answers. We have to trust that God will guide our steps and equip us with what we need. So, what does it look like to shift our perspective back to our certain hope in Christ?

One of the most effective ways to keep our focus on Jesus and His promises is to surround ourselves with the truth of God's Word. Read Scripture daily. Write specific verses out and keep them on your mirror, your dashboard, or above your kitchen sink—places where you will see them often. Invite people into your life who will speak the truth of God's Word into your circumstances. Cultivating rhythms of remembering is essential to keeping our eyes fixed on the hope we have in Christ and our faith in Him always growing.

If you take nothing else from our time today, hear this—Jesus Christ is our hope fulfilled (Luke 24:27; Rom. 8:1-4), and that hope changes everything about our everyday. When I really let that truth sink in, it makes me want to respond like the shepherds after they found Mary, Joseph, and the baby just as the angels said they would.

> READ LUKE 2:17 AND 2:20. **How did the shepherds respond to finding the Savior?**

Do you find yourself sharing the good news of the gospel with others often? If not, what holds you back? Identify one person in your life with whom you could share the gospel this Advent season, and write down a plan for doing so.

The more familiar things become to us, like the details of the Christmas story, the more they lose their sense of wonder in our hearts and minds. The Advent season moves so quickly that it can be hard to slow down long enough to see the reminders of this hope all around us. Take some time this week to create a tangible reminder of the hope—the very life for today and eternity—you have in Christ; this could be a sticky note on your mirror, an art print on your wall, or a reminder you set in your phone. Also make a point to send a note of encouragement to someone who you know needs it this time of year.

May we be reminders to one another this season that our hope has been fulfilled in Christ.

DAY 4

BELIEVE IN GOD'S PROMISES

by Amanda Mae Steele

Do you have a bucket list of "must dos" for your lifetime? If you do, either in your head or on paper, it likely includes a big ticket item or two—something like an exotic trip, meeting a celebrity, or starting a family of your own. Maybe it's something exhilarating like hiking Mount Everest, starting a business, or building a school in a rural area of the Philippines.

As I'm writing this, my dad has been in the hospital for more than a week. At times we've been unsure if he'll make it, but he's resolved to fight for his life and stick around for at least the next few months. He hopes to check off one more of his bucket list items—the arrival of my first child and his first grandchild, something he has anticipated for nearly a decade.

A decade seems like a long time to wait for something specific, but in the Bible we read about another man who spent a lot longer waiting for someone's arrival—the arrival of the Messiah, to be exact.

READ LUKE 2:25-35.

How is Simeon described in this passage? What was unique about him and his relationship with God, that he was able to identify the child Jesus as the promised Messiah?

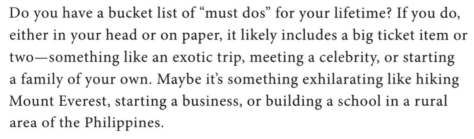

Shortly after Jesus was born, Joseph and Mary took Him to the temple as part of the Jewish rituals that followed a child's birth. While there, they met a man named Simeon who is described as "righteous and devout" (v. 25). The text tells us he was "looking forward to Israel's consolation," another way of saying he was waiting for God to deliver on His promise to save His people. We also read that the presence of the Holy Spirit was with Simeon, and the Spirit revealed to Simeon that he would meet the Messiah. Talk about a bucket list item!

Jesus promised that the Father would send the Holy Spirit to indwell believers after He left (Acts 1:1-9; 2:1-4). But prior to that event, we read about times when the Holy Spirit came upon certain individuals to reveal God's truth to them. This was the case with Simeon, and it was also the case with another man involved in the Christmas story.

READ LUKE 1:57-79.

We've met this prophet before. What did the filling of the Holy Spirit lead Zechariah to do?

Similarly to Simeon, Zechariah was described as "righteous in God's sight" (Luke 1:6). The Holy Spirit led Zechariah to prophesy about his son, John, and how he would prepare the way for Jesus. The same Spirit led Simeon to the temple when Joseph, Mary, and Jesus would also be there, and the same Spirit gave Simeon the ability to affirm Jesus' identity as God's Promised One.

READ LUKE 2:28-35.

Circle the phrases Simeon used to describe Jesus in verses 29-32. What do you learn about Jesus from these descriptions?

Pay close attention to verses 31-32. Who is God's salvation for?

When Simeon met Jesus, he described Him as "your [God's] salvation" (v. 30), "a light for revelation to the Gentiles" (v. 32), and "glory to your people Israel." In other words, Jesus is hope for all people! As Dr. David Jeremiah notes on verse 32 in *The Jeremiah Study Bible,* "Apart from the Spirit of God, an orthodox first-century Jew would never have looked at the Messiah and turned His blessing to the Gentiles, for the Jews believed the Messiah would come for Israel alone."[3] Jesus was much more than just the "consolation of Israel" that Simeon anticipated. It's no wonder Joseph and Mary marveled at the things Simeon was saying.

Imagine yourself as a first-century Jew, present at the temple that day hearing the message that God was bringing salvation to all the world. What questions might you have? What does the fact that salvation is for all people teach you about God?

READ LUKE 2:36-38.

Simeon wasn't the only person excited to meet Jesus that day in the temple. In Kristi McLelland's study, *Jesus and Women,* she shares that one of the unique things about the Gospel of Luke is, "We see twenty-seven pairings of spiritual teachings and Jesus' actions . . . one featuring a man, and the other featuring a woman."[4] We are witnessing it right here today with the parallel stories of Simeon and another faithful elderly saint Anna. (One of my favorites!)

What are some similarities between Simeon and Anna? Jot them down on this chart.

SIMEON	ANNA

Like Simeon, Anna was old, and like Simeon, Anna was a faithful servant of God. Anna spent all of her time in the temple, where she worshiped God, fasted, and prayed. This woman's devotion to God is admirable, and God rewarded it by including her among the few people who first met Jesus.

How did Anna respond when she encountered the child?

Anna's response to meeting Jesus fell right in line with what we know about her: she praised God and shared about Jesus with others. Can you imagine being at the temple that day and hearing from not one but two prophets that the child Jesus was indeed the Messiah? What a monumental moment in both Simeon's and Anna's lives! Both of them had faithfully dedicated their lives to loving and serving the Lord, and God granted both of them the privilege of getting to meet and share about the one true Messiah.

The hopes of Simeon and Anna were fulfilled that day when they met Jesus, and they responded by praising God for His gift and sharing the great news. If you have accepted Christ as your Savior, then you know how good this news is, and you have the indwelling of the Spirit and the ability to share the hope of His salvation, too.

Both Anna and Simeon positioned themselves to encounter God by being in the temple and being open to the guidance of the Holy Spirit. How are you positioning yourself to encounter Jesus this season?

Yesterday, you identified at least one person you know who needs the hope Jesus has to offer, someone who needs to hear that they are dearly loved by God and that salvation is for him or her, too. Pray for that person (or people!) now, and take your first step toward reaching out to them.

May we be women who boldly praise God and share the hope of Jesus this season. May we be women who are willing and ready to follow God's lead and who experience the joy of His presence, just as Simeon and Anna did on that day more than two thousand years ago.

DAY 5

BELIEVE IN GOD'S SOVEREIGNTY

by Carol Pipes

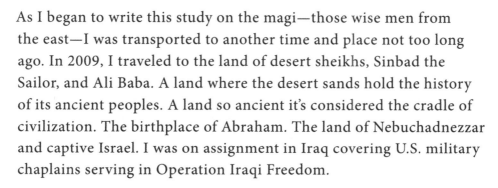

As I began to write this study on the magi—those wise men from the east—I was transported to another time and place not too long ago. In 2009, I traveled to the land of desert sheikhs, Sinbad the Sailor, and Ali Baba. A land where the desert sands hold the history of its ancient peoples. A land so ancient it's considered the cradle of civilization. The birthplace of Abraham. The land of Nebuchadnezzar and captive Israel. I was on assignment in Iraq covering U.S. military chaplains serving in Operation Iraqi Freedom.

This was my first trip to the Middle East, and I marveled at the barren land surrounding the first military base we visited. Beyond the metal fence and concertina wire lay the desert—stretches of sand for miles, with dust clouds whirling across the surface. Surveying the landscape, I imagined Bedouin tribes traveling by caravan on their desert ships. Perhaps even the wise men had traversed this very spot some two thousand years before.

I'll never forget those chilly nights in the desert looking at the great expanse of the heavens above me. The stars seemed brighter, closer, and more numerous in that desert sky. The words of God's promise to Abraham came alive to me in that place: "I will indeed bless you and make your offspring as numerous as the stars of the sky and the sand on the seashore. Your offspring will possess the city gates of their enemies. And all the nations of the earth will be blessed by your offspring because you have obeyed my command" (Gen. 22:17-18).

In the days of Abraham, the time of the wise men, and still today, "the heavens declare the glory of God" (Ps. 19:1). I never could've imagined God would send me to Iraq. But isn't that just like God? His plan for our lives is beyond our dreams and imaginings. In today's session, we'll look at the hope found in God's powerful presence and providence.

> **On a blank piece of paper or in your journal, write down what you know about the magi who visited Jesus. Do this before you read today's Scripture passage.**

Compare the facts revealed about the magi in Matthew 2:1–12 with the notes you wrote down.

This passage about the magi contains no shortage of mysteries. Who were these wise men from the east? Scripture doesn't give us much information. Were they kings as the popular Christmas song supposes, and were there only three of them? Biblical scholars have offered a few theories on their origin and profession. Perhaps they were Persian philosophers or Arabian statesmen. Or maybe they were Babylonian astrologers who were schooled in the ancient Hebrew manuscripts passed down from the days of Daniel when he was chief governor over all the wise men in Babylon (Dan. 2:48).

We don't know exactly where they came from or how many were in the caravan. But here's what we do know: The wise men saw an unfamiliar star at its first rising, and they knew it meant something. Curiosity piqued, then they set out on a long journey.

And what about that supernatural star? A star moved across the sky and led the magi to Jesus. That's one amazing celestial event. Scholars have debated the origin of the star, as well. Was it an alignment of planets? Or maybe a comet with a really long tail? But let's not rule out the possibility that the God of the universe created a magnificent star for this specific purpose. No matter the star's origin, it was a miracle, nonetheless. In His perfect timing, God worked supernaturally to lead these men to Jesus.

Matthew tells us the wise men's journey led them to Jerusalem, where they started asking around, "Where is he who has been born king of the Jews?" (Matt. 2:2). The magi connected the celestial event to the birth of a king. Some scholars believe these wise men had access to ancient manuscripts, including the Old Testament prophecies, and associated the star with the birth of the long-awaited Jewish Messiah. For example, Numbers 24:17 records Balaam's prophecy, "I see him, but not now; I perceive him, but not near. A star will come from Jacob, and a scepter will arise from Israel." King Herod heard about their inquiries and was worried. Matthew says Herod was deeply disturbed, and all of Jerusalem was disturbed with him (Matt. 2:3).

Why do you think King Herod was disturbed? What about the citizens of Jerusalem? Why might the arrival of the wise men have been disconcerting?

Herod was most likely anxious because he knew he wasn't the rightful heir to the throne of Israel. He had aligned himself with Rome politically and was given rule of Judea in exchange for his loyalty. Now the promised Messiah threatened his position and Rome's power.

Herod had no idea where the Messiah was supposed to be born. He gathered the chief priests and scribes—those considered experts in the Old Testament Law—and asked them for the location. Citing a prophecy in Micah 5:2, they told Herod the Messiah would come from Bethlehem. Sneaky Herod then met secretly with the wise men and manipulated their trust. He even got them to reveal the exact time the star appeared. (He would use this info later in a horrific act of power and paranoia.) Herod sent the magi to Bethlehem, saying "Go and search carefully for the child. When you find him, report back to me so that I too can go and worship him" (v. 8).

The wise men left Herod and, lo and behold, there was that star of wonder again! Matthew wrote, "When they saw the star, they were overwhelmed with joy" (v. 10). The star led them directly to Jesus.

When the wise men found Jesus with Mary, they fell to the ground and worshiped Him. They gave Him expensive gifts fit for a king—gold, frankincense, and myrrh. Little did they know how valuable those gifts would be to this lowly family. Those extravagant gifts most likely provided the means for Joseph, Mary, and Jesus to flee to Egypt and escape Herod's treacherous plan to kill the newborn King (Matt. 2:16-18).

Recall a time when you witnessed the supernatural power of God at work in your life. Write about it below and describe the joy you felt.

After they saw and worshiped Jesus, the wise men were warned in a dream not to go back to Herod. Scripture tells us they returned to their home country by another route, avoiding Herod and his evil plot. And that's the last we hear of these mysterious magi.

As we already noted, there's a fair amount of mystery in this passage. A supernatural star, mysterious men from a distant land, unexpected gifts that came just in the nick of time, and a divine dream that circumvented a second meeting with a crazed king. This story is a reminder that God's ways aren't our ways, and His plans rarely fit into a nice, neat little package that we can comprehend. But God has a plan and a provision for our salvation, of that we can be sure.

How does reading about God's provision in this passage offer you hope?

How does it help you trust Him when His ways seem strange?

READ PSALM 119:105.

God provided a light for the wise men to find Jesus, and He provides a light for us on our own spiritual journey. God's Word reveals the hope found in the finished work of Christ on the cross.

As you wrap up today's reading, think of a specific time from this past week when you experienced God's presence with you. If you can't think of anything, ask God to open your eyes to the many ways He is present in your life; ask Him to guide your every step.

PAPER STARS

by Lauren Ervin

One of the most important things we learn from the story of Jesus' birth is that the hope of the gospel is for everyone. The host of angels appeared to lowly shepherds. Likewise, the star didn't appear to the scholars and scribes of Jerusalem. Instead, it was shown to Gentile magi who devout Jews would have considered to be pagans. The Father announced His Son's birth to the most unlikely candidates, showing His love for all of humanity and His desire for all to know Him. As you make this star and display it in your home, use it as a reminder to thank God for your hopes that are fulfilled in Jesus and to share about Him with others.

GATHER

- Lunch bags
- Large glue sticks (or hot glue)
- Scissors
- Hole punch
- String

DIRECTIONS

Count out seven bags.

Add glue to the flat face of the first bag. Place a second bag on top facing the same direction and press down to make sure they stick together. Repeat this with all the bags.

Once you have all of your bags secured together with your glue, cut the top into a pointed shape.

Add in any center cuts as desired. Test to make sure it can open completely.

Add glue to the flat face of the top bag. Open up the bag and press it to the other loose end to form a star. Hold until the glue dries.

PERFECT TIMING

by Karen Daniel

"When the fullness of time had come, God sent forth his son ..." (Gal. 4:4, ESV). Hundreds of years had passed since God's people last heard from Him, yet they remained hopeful for the Savior He had promised. As always, God's timing was perfect.

Take a minute to recall with your teen the last bit of good news he or she received. Talk through such questions as:

- Who delivered it?
- What was it about?
- Where were they when they heard it?
- Why was it such good news?
- And lastly, when did the good news come? Was it too early, too late, or right on time?

It's never too late to receive good news, and that's what happened the night the angel proclaimed Jesus' birth to the shepherds.

READ LUKE 2:8-20 WITH YOUR TEEN THIS WEEK.

Grab some colored pencils. As you read the passage together, do a little investigative journalism and walk through the same five Ws using the following guide:

1. **WHO:** Circle in yellow who brought the good news as well as who it was for.

2. **WHEN:** Underline in blue the time of day when the angel appeared.

3. **WHERE:** Place a green box around where the shepherds were when they heard the news.

4. **WHAT:** Place purple brackets around the good news the angel delivered.

5. **WHY:** Highlight in red the reason for the good news.

At long last, God sent the Savior He had promised. But He didn't send Jesus just for the people of that day; Jesus was sent for all of us. God cares just as much about your life and the things going on in our world today as He did about the shepherds and people of Jesus' time.

Take time as a family to identify who you know who needs to hear the good news of Luke 2. Mark a time on your calendar as you decide who you will share with, when you will meet them, and where you will go. It could even be as simple as inviting a few of your unchurched friends over to bake Christmas cookies. In your time together, play some Christmas music and talk about some of the ways—but especially the reason—you celebrate Christ's birth.

MAKE DESSERT!

by Bekah Stoneking

If you want warm, delicious cookies, you have to find and mix the ingredients, roll the dough into balls, place them into the oven, and wait. Your tummy might start growling and you might feel like the cookies are taking forever to bake, but you trust that soon they'll be ready to eat. Why do you trust this? Because you can smell them baking! You have proof that delicious cookies are coming.

READ LUKE 1:5-24.

As Zechariah and Elizabeth grew older, they thought it would be impossible to have a baby. Then, God made the impossible happen. Elizabeth was going to have a son! A little while later, Elizabeth was visited by her family member, Mary. Something impossible was also happening to Mary. She was going to have a baby, too!

After years of waiting, God answered Elizabeth's prayers in a new way. At just the right time, God gave Elizabeth a baby. Elizabeth's hope was finally fulfilled, which gave encouragement to Mary while she prepared to have baby Jesus. Anything is possible with God, and God always keeps His promises.

ACTIVITY

Gather the ingredients for one of your child's favorite baked treats, like cookies, brownies, or banana bread.

Pre-heat the oven and work together to follow the recipe. While your dessert is baking, brainstorm ways God has kept His promises, answered prayers, or blessed people. You can recall examples from your favorite Bible stories, or you can name examples from the lives of your family and friends.

As you smell your dessert baking, have your child write or draw about one of the examples you brainstormed, or use an electronic device to make a recording telling the story of how God showed His faithfulness.

PRAY

Thank You, God, for the delicious food You have given us to enjoy. Thank You for all of the ways You have proven Your goodness to us. Help us to trust You always and to tell others faithfully about Your promises. Amen.

Look, your King
is coming
to you

Rejoice greatly, Daughter
Zion! Shout in triumph,
Daughter Jerusalem! Look,
your King is coming to
you; he is righteous and
victorious, humble and
riding on a donkey, on
a colt, the foal of a donkey.

ZECHARIAH 9:9

Hope
Deferred

THE DISCIPLES' WAIT

by Sarah Doss

For the first two weeks of our study together, we've focused on the threads of promise and hope that run through Scripture in general and through the Christmas story in particular. These examples highlight God's care for His children and show us how His glory is at work for our good. We've mostly studied passages of the Bible that seem to have some closure or semblance of a "happy ending." Sure, none of the people who we've discussed were perfect, but we've seen God use them mightily to further His kingdom.

But what about the Bible passages where God's providence is less obvious or maybe even seems lacking? How does the Bible counsel us to persevere when met with evil, suffering, and sickness? How do we keep our hearts encouraged in the Lord when the ravages of the fall shade every relationship, joy, hope, thought, and intent of our hearts? In a nutshell, how do we keep steady faith with what Proverbs 13:12 would call a "hope deferred" (ESV)?

In the Advent season, our default is to focus on the joy of Christ's coming, not parts of the story like Herod's edict to kill male babies, which overwhelmed a town with grief and threatened the safety of baby Jesus. It's easy to let our thoughts dwell on all of the fulfilled hopes we have in Jesus and forget the political, racial, and religious tensions that the Old Testament world felt as they waited for the Messiah. However, the Bible is full of polarities—good and evil, light and darkness, hope and despair—and that is true even within the Christmas story. This means the good news of Jesus' birth also has much to teach us about navigating our broken world and answering some of those "but how" questions above.

It'd be foolish to suggest easy answers to the problem of evil in this world. And God doesn't necessarily explain the "why" of every hurt or injustice to us. But God does help us learn how to look beyond them. Consider the perspective shift Paul encouraged in Romans 5:1-5, printed on the next page.

> Therefore, since we have been justified by faith, we have peace with God through our Lord Jesus Christ. We have also obtained access through him by faith into this grace in which we stand, and we boast in the hope of the glory of God. And not only that, but we also boast in our afflictions, because we know that affliction produces endurance, endurance produces proven character, and proven character produces hope. This hope will not disappoint us, because God's love has been poured out in our hearts through the Holy Spirit who was given to us.

Did you catch that? Because "nothing will be impossible with God" (Luke 1:37), He is able to produce hope from suffering. Romans 5 reminds us that God never turns a blind eye to the suffering of His children or to the evil in the world. But He somehow uses it to produce endurance, character, and hope in the deep places of their hearts.

This doesn't minimize the hurt of painful experiences or our call to be agents for reconciliation on this earth, but it does help us wrestle with the apparent chasm between God's declarations of love for us and the difficulties we find ourselves experiencing here on earth.

Theologian J. I. Packer said it this way, "If you ask, 'Why is this happening?' no light may come, but if you ask, 'How am I to glorify God now?' there will always be an answer."[1] The why of evil isn't always readily available to us. But there's always a way for us to glorify God even in the midst of injustice and inequity here on earth.

Today we find ourselves caught in the middle of the already but not yet of salvation history. Hope has come in Jesus, which made a way for us to have eternal peace with God, but ultimate restoration is still ahead. The Bible validates this reality for us: "For in subjecting everything to him, he left nothing that is not subject to him" (Heb. 2:8b). God is in fact sovereign over all things, even though all of the injustice we witness on earth may make that hard to see. The fulfillment of our hope may be deferred for now, but hope is our inheritance and our ultimate end. For a time we may try to grasp lasting hope only to find that it slips through our fingers time and time again. But one day that will be no more. One day we'll reap our full inheritance, and we "will shine like the sun in [our] Father's kingdom" (Matt. 13:43a).

We'll get to more on our eternal hope next week. For now, let's examine some of the "unjust" stories we see in the first-century world, how God uses those difficult stories for His purposes in spite of the circumstances, and the certainty we have in God's righteous right arm to one day set these situations right. He's still working even when we're not sure how.

1 | Are you someone who tends to approach the hard things in life head on, or do you prefer to ignore or run away from them? How does this impact your relationships with those close to you? How have you seen it impact your relationship with God?

2 | Share about a time in your life or a specific circumstance when God used pain or suffering to bring about His good purpose. Describe what it was like to walk through that difficult season, as well as what you now see God taught you through the process.

3 | Read aloud Romans 5:1-5. Discuss the connection between suffering, endurance, character, and hope.

4 | Take a few minutes to share some of the Bible verses or stories from Scripture that you cling to when hope seems hard to come by. Explain why these passages are important to you.

5 | Before you pray together, discuss the hard things going on in your lives at this time. Partner up the group, and encourage them to check in on and support one another during the coming weeks.

NOTES

LOOK TO PROMISES KEPT

by Ashley Marivittori Gorman

Last week gave us so much hope, didn't it? We saw all the ways Jesus' birth proved to be the fulfillment of past Old Testament prophecies, and all the unlikely people God used to play a part along the way. Jesus—the Shepherd, the Messiah, the Lamb, the virgin's Son, the King who the wisest of men bowed before, the Redeemer of Israel—had finally come. After such a long season of waiting, God's promised Deliverer arrived just like God said He would.

As we read last week, Matthew focuses much of his birth narrative on the visit from the magi. By the time we come to Matthew 2:16, some important events have transpired in just the two or so short years Jesus has been alive.

READ MATTHEW 2:13-15.

Herod learned through the magi about some age-old prophecies foretelling the birth of a Jewish King, and he wasn't happy about them. Herod's strategy to resolve the issue was to kill the child, but that meant he needed to learn where the child was located. So, he asked the magi to give him the coordinates of Jesus once they found Him. However, the men were warned in a dream to avoid Herod and return home by a different route. They obeyed. Joseph also received a dream-warning from God by way of an angel who instructed him to take Jesus and Mary to Egypt, far away from Herod and his murderous plan.

Though the whole ordeal seems like God is winning by the skin of His teeth, coming up with eleventh-hour solutions to thwart Herod's plans, verse 15 closes by telling us otherwise.

What do these verses reveal about God's ultimate and specific purpose in all these events?

In verse 15, Matthew connected the Israelites' time in Egypt with Jesus' through words from the prophet Hosea, who wrote: "When Israel was a child, I loved him, and out of Egypt I called my son" (Hos. 11:1). Nothing surprises God. In fact, He was in control the entire time, using the real-time events to do something very specific.

READ MATTHEW 2:16-18.

Describe the state of Herod's heart in your own words below. Consider things like where he likely found security and value, what he was afraid of, what might have brought him comfort, or what primary emotion probably ruled his heart.

Herod waited and waited, and eventually he realized he was outwitted by the magi. That little boy was still out there somewhere, a threat to his rule. What follows is the most tragic scene in the Christmas story, an event known to history as "the massacre of the innocents." Thinking he had the power and cleverness to sabotage the plans of all-knowing, all-powerful, all-wise God yet again, Herod slaughtered a town's worth of little boys in Bethlehem and beyond, ages two and under (the age Jesus probably was). Can you imagine the confusion? The heartbreak? The loss? These families had no idea a larger story was going on—and even if they had known, that knowledge wouldn't have lessened their pain.

A group of boys in that little town, gone. The words from the prophet Jeremiah in verse 18 paint a picture of unbearable grief and mourning. I can only imagine those mothers crying out, "Where are you, God?"

READ MATTHEW 2:17-18 AGAIN. **Take note of what these verses reveal about Herod's action.**

Verse 18 is a quotation from the prophet Jeremiah, where he personified the mothers of Israel as "Rachel." Back in Genesis, during the age of the patriarchs, Rachel was the wife of Jacob. Her sons—Joseph and Benjamin—were threatened with being "no more" as they were carried away into Egypt (Gen. 42:36, ESV). Many years later, the children of Israel were taken from their land and carried off into exile, and Jeremiah described their mothers in similar language. Like Rachel's sons, they too were mourned over bitterly "because they are no more," rendering Israel a barren, dead nation (Jer. 31:15). The grief was so deep in Jeremiah's day, he spoke as if the loss was felt by Rachel herself.

Fast forward to the time of Christ, and Matthew used the same text to reveal that yet another part of Israel's story would be both fulfilled and restored in Christ. Yes, "Rachel" cried out into the night, a city of mothers doubled over in pain. But all those voices rising up above the city—they weren't meaningless. A parent's voice crying out over the death of a son was a signal—a signal with equal importance as every other prophecy about Christ—that the Messiah was here.

As we've all experienced by now, the joyful and pleasant moments aren't the only things that fulfill the purposes of God in this world. The dark ones count for something, too. They matter. There's something going on with them—God is doing something in the shadows—even if we don't have any answers.

We can all agree this isn't the sort of story we want to tell at Christmastime. We want to remember the bright things: Jesus, the light of the world. Jesus is the light of the world, yes, but He is the light *who shines into the darkness.*

Jesus wasn't born into a greeting card or a quaint nativity scene, where hot chocolate simmers on the iron stove behind the manger and classic Christmas songs hang in the air. No, our Savior was born into the real world, and it's a dark one. The world of you and me, of sin and brokenness. A world where massacres happen, where people are so blinded by the false promises of power and prestige that they're literally willing to kill. A world with all its mourning and its problems and its Herods. With mothers who still weep and mourn and question the ways of God.

The darkness can seem unbearable, but the good news for us is this: Even Herod-level darkness didn't scare Jesus off from coming to us. Yes, King Herod brought many sons to their grave, but this King? He will bring many sons to glory.

Fill in the chart below, using the references from Matthew 2 as your guide.

VERSE	ORIGINAL PROPHECY	HOW IT WAS FULFILLED
Matthew 2:5-6	Ruler/King out of Bethlehem	Jesus born in Bethlehem
Matthew 2:16	Slew children	→
Matthew 2:17-18	Weeping refused to be comforted	
Matthew 2:23	Called a Nazarene	lived in Nazareth

Considering these verses, what major point do you think Matthew was trying to make about the birth of Christ?

The circumstances surrounding Jesus' birth and early childhood are wrought with constant complications and plot twists. At almost every juncture, all hope seemed lost, or at least deferred—a virgin mother, no sufficient place to be born, a murderous king, evacuation to Egypt. Yet, at those very junctures, in the middle of the chaos and the darkness, Scriptures are fulfilled. This clearly shows us that our God—He's King. No one can undo His will, thwart His plans, or outmaneuver Him.

Herod tried. As we saw, he delusionally attempted to interrupt God's plans. Yet at every point, he played right into the hands of God, creating the very circumstances by which a prophecy would be fulfilled. Each step of trying to kill the Christ played out as fulfillment for His coming.

Herod's story leaves us reflecting on two important truths. One: God has all authority over any enemy, and though it seems our hope may be deferred, it's only temporary. His plan will end up working. Even when we feel like Rachel, crying into the night, the pieces really will fall into place. God is omniscient, turning things for good. He always has been.

What situation(s) do you need to lay at the Lord's feet today, trusting Him to put the pieces in place and overcome the enemy?

Two: Jesus is the Son of God, King of the Jews, Ruler of heaven and Earth, Savior of the world, Messiah foretold. And He's not merely King. He's a *different sort* of King. He doesn't come killing others in order to rule; He comes dying for them. His ascent to a throne isn't through deceit or murder. It's through truth-telling and self-sacrifice. When it comes to those who might rebel against His authority or rule, He isn't out for blood. Instead, He sheds His own for them. He doesn't try to side-step the plan of God; He obeys it. Jesus isn't like earthly leaders. He's altogether different. This is our King. Born into darkness. Light of the world.

Why is it important that we understand the situations around Jesus' birth were full of complication, confusion, darkness, and deferred hope? What difference does this truth make for you today?

Spend some time in solitude and reflection, letting your thoughts dwell on the light of Christ and His impact on our sin-darkened world.

LOOK TO GOD'S WORD

by Susan M. Hill

If you've been a follower of Jesus for any length of time, then there's a good chance you've wrestled through seasons when hope seems lost or God's plans seem confusing. During a long season of hardship, maybe you've wondered if you misunderstood God, or you've been tempted to believe He's forgotten you. Perhaps you've felt so low you've doubted God and wondered if Jesus is who He says He is. If that's true, you find yourself in excellent company because John the Baptist knew the feeling.

READ MATTHEW 11:1-19.

If you recall from last week, John the Baptist was the cousin of Jesus, born to Elizabeth and Zechariah and destined to be the prophet who prepared people for the coming of the Messiah. By all accounts, John obeyed God and did everything possible to fulfill his calling. John wasn't a glory hound attempting to bask in the spotlight. When speaking about Jesus, he said, "He must increase, but I must decrease" (John 3:30). Jesus spoke so highly of John that He said, "Truly I tell you, among those born of women no one greater than John the Baptist has appeared, but the least in the kingdom of heaven is greater than he" (Matt. 11:11). Scripture makes it clear—John was the prophet God called him to be. And yet, in Matthew 11, we find John experiencing a season of suffering that filled him with doubts.

Look closely at Matthew 11:2-3. In your own words, what was bothering John?

John's trouble started when Herod had him arrested and put in prison because of Herodias, his brother Philip's wife. John told him that it wasn't lawful for him to be in a relationship with her (Matt. 14:3-4). John was speaking the truth—but it cost him. The passage doesn't say so, but it's reasonable to believe that as John waited in prison, he retraced his steps and played the events over and over again in his mind trying to make sense of his calling, his expectations for the Messiah, and the reality of Jesus' ministry to date. The text doesn't tell us when, but at some point, John began to question whether Jesus was who He claimed to be. From John's perspective, it was a legitimate question. After all, John had done everything right and ended up in prison, sidelined from his ministry, isolated from other believers, physically tormented, and spiritually discouraged. And so, John sent word to Jesus' disciples and requested that they ask Jesus, "Are you the one who is to come, or should we expect someone else?" (Matt. 11:3).

Questions are prone to creep in when Jesus doesn't meet our expectations. Keep in mind that as a prophet, John the Baptist believed Jesus to be the Messiah who was sent to "proclaim liberty to the captives and freedom to the prisoners" (Isa. 61:1), and yet John sat in prison. To complicate matters, John had prophesied that Christ would bring judgment, but the Roman government remained intact (Matt. 3:11-12). Meanwhile, Jesus was preaching to sinners and teaching about forgiveness while Rome continued to call the shots, and political and religious corruption was running rampant. From John's limited viewpoint, things weren't going as planned.

Are there areas in your life where Jesus hasn't met your expectations since you started following Him? If so, explain.

What John didn't realize (and often we don't either) is that he was too much in the thick of the action to see the bigger picture. Jesus' followers anticipated a new and improved political regime, and when that didn't come, they began to lose hope. They didn't realize God was ushering in a different type of kingdom. One that would reconcile sinners to God and allow us to spend eternity with Him. One that was so much better than the earthly kingdom they desired. Jesus' followers found themselves in the already but not yet, the in-between we remain in until Jesus returns to finish setting everything right.

We have more in common with John the Baptist than we might think. Sure, most of us haven't landed in prison in the midst of pursuing our callings, but we can all relate to John's state of mind when he summoned the disciples to question Jesus. We've all experienced problems that have caused us to doubt Jesus and His mission. And when Jesus doesn't respond to our struggle in the way we think He should, we're inclined to question Him. Like John, our perspective is limited. We look at our circumstances through the lens of the here and now. God looks at things through the lens of eternity.

The question remains, though: How do we deal with doubt while we wait for this deferred hope we are promised? We listen to Jesus. Jesus gave us the answer when He responded to John's question brought to Him by the disciples. Jesus replied to them, "Go and report to John what you hear and see: The blind receive their sight, the lame walk, those with leprosy are cleansed, the deaf hear, the dead are raised, and the poor are told the good news" (Matt. 11:4-5).

To offset John's doubt, Jesus pointed John back to the Scriptures. In Jesus' response to the disciples, He used phrases found in the Book of Isaiah to describe the work He had been doing and demonstrate He was indeed the Messiah (Isa. 35:6; 61:1).[2] John was an avid student of the Scriptures, and Jesus' words would've prompted John to make the connection back to the Old Testament prophecies. John would've connected the dots and been reassured that Jesus was who He claimed to be and would do as He promised. To be sure, John was still in a challenging situation. But having the encouragement that God's Word is true is what John needed to keep going despite his difficult circumstances.

In which area(s) of your life are you most inclined to question God's plans? With that specific circumstance in mind, how much is influenced by your current circumstances? Does a shift to an eternal perspective change anything for you?

Read the following Scriptures to help build your confidence in God's plans and promises. Pick at least one to commit to memory. Add your own to the list!

- ISAIAH 26:3-4 *Everlasting Rock*
- EPHESIANS 2:1-10 *By grace have been saved.*
- HEBREWS 4:14-16 *Received mercy & find grace.*
- REVELATION 21:1-5 *Wipe away every tear.*
- _____
- _____

As we wait for God's promises to be fulfilled in our own lives, we too, will need to rely on the Scriptures to deal with our doubt. Apart from God's Word, we default to a lifestyle of diminished faith. But if we make it a priority to spend time in God's Word, we'll be continually reassured that Jesus is who He claimed to be, and a time is coming when He will do everything He promised. We don't have to understand everything about our situation if we are convinced that He is good.

LOOK BEYOND YOUR EXPECTATIONS

by Yvonne Faith Russell

Have you ever waited for years in anticipation of something? As a girl, did you anxiously await a milestone birthday, senior prom, or high school graduation? Have you longed for a dream job, a husband, or motherhood (or all of the above!)? What about waiting years to have a certain prayer answered? I assume the answer is yes to something. Longing is a shared part of the human experience.

The longer we wait for something, the more we tend to imagine exactly what it will be like. But both Scripture and personal experience teach us that if we expect things to be a certain way, then we can fail to see the fulfillment of what we've been waiting and praying for. This is not unlike what happened to the Samaritan woman when she met the Messiah at a drinking well.

READ JOHN 4:1-26.

Before reading on, make a list of the things that stand out to you from the John 4 passage.

Imagine growing up hearing prophecies about the long-awaited Messiah. Imagine your mother brushing your hair while telling you a story about the Savior of the world who was to come. Perhaps at the dinner table you discussed the coming of the Anointed One, or right before bed your father told you a story about the promised King. Undoubtedly you created a picture of Him in your mind. What would He look like? What would He sound like? What would He wear? In your child-like imagination, He most likely would not look like an ordinary man. Perhaps He looked spectacular, effervescent, and most certainly recognizable.

John 4 introduces us to a Samaritan woman drawing water from a well in the heat of the day, long after the other women have drawn from the well (most likely an attempt to avoid the shame of her relational history, which comes to light later on). While she was drawing the water, a Jewish man—Jesus—approached her and asked her for a drink. In this single action, Jesus shattered two major social constructions of the day.

John 4:3-4 tells us that Jesus was traveling from Judea to Galilee, but He needed to go through Samaria. Samaria was located directly in the middle of the two regions, so crossing through Samaria might not seem out of the ordinary. However, most Jews opted to take a longer route to Galilee simply to avoid traveling through Samaria because the Jews and the Samaritans didn't associate with each other. Jesus broke the social norm of the day by not only traveling through Samaria but stopping to talk to a Samaritan woman. Both a Jew associating with a Samaritan and a man speaking to a woman in public were unheard of during this time in Middle Eastern history. You can almost hear the surprise in her voice when the Samaritan woman replied in John 4:9, "How is it that You, a Jew, ask for a drink from me, a Samaritan woman?"

Jesus responded, "If you knew the gift of God, and who is saying to you, 'Give me a drink,' you would ask him, and he would give you living water" (v. 10). Jesus went on to explain that He is the living water and the source of eternal life and salvation. That she was a Samaritan and a woman did not matter. To Jesus, she was simply a sinner, and He was there to save her soul.

The woman didn't understand that her hope was in front of her. Nor did she understand Jesus' offer to quench her spiritual thirst; she still thought they were talking about water. "Sir, give me this water so that I won't get thirsty and come here to draw water," she says.

> **Can you relate to the Samaritan woman at this point in her story? Is there a distinct time in your past when you failed to see how God was meeting your spiritual need because you were preoccupied with your physical needs and natural desires?**

Jesus didn't scorn the Samaritan woman for her lack of understanding. Instead, He continued to patiently reveal Himself to the woman. In verses 16-18, Jesus asked the woman to call her husband, subsequently revealing that she has had five husbands, and the man she was living with was not her husband. Jesus revealed her history so that He could reveal Himself. The woman saw the supernatural, all-knowing aspect of Jesus and identified Him as a prophet, undoubtedly stirring her own hopes of the Messiah—that He would be coming soon (v. 25).

Imagine the woman's surprise when she finds out that the Man who asked her to draw water was the Messiah her people had been waiting for—God Himself on earth, and

He was talking to her! Perhaps she didn't recognize Him because He didn't fit the image of the Messiah that she created in her mind. Maybe she failed to recognize Him because she was expecting a different message. She clearly stated, "He will explain everything to us" (v. 25). One can only wonder what type of explanation she was waiting for.

In this way we can all relate to the Samaritan woman. Our preconceived notions or unrealistic expectations blind us to the ways God is answering our prayers, to the point that we don't believe He's at work because it doesn't look or sound like what we expected. The Messiah who she had heard about, who she was waiting for, was standing in front of her. How many times have we waited for something that was right in front of us?

This Advent season, like many seasons in our lives, can feel like a season of waiting—for unfulfilled longings, deferred hope, promises yet to be kept. Even as we wait though, God continues to provide. And quite often, He provides in a way we aren't expecting. Our hope has come, and although we continue to look forward to His second coming, we know that God has already provided strength to sustain us on our journey, and the hope we have in Him is an anchor for our soul (Heb. 6:19).

> Set aside some time today for reflective prayer. Ask yourself:
>
> 1. Are there areas in my life where I need to look beyond my expectations to see specific ways God is at work?
>
> 2. What misplaced anticipations are keeping me from seeing God's answers and provisions?
>
> 3. Where have I been too focused on my natural desires to see God trying to meet a spiritual need in my life?

As you reflect, thank God for His patience and His desire to reveal Himself in your life. And thank Him that He delivers hope even in ways we aren't expecting. Ask God to open your eyes to see His provision and answers to what you've prayed for.

LOOK FOR PURPOSE TODAY

by Erin Franklin

For many people, going first and not being left behind is an inherent desire. When my cousin was about three years old, her older brother (who was only about five at the time), had gotten to do another thing "first." My aunt recounts that this particular episode threw my youngest cousin over the edge in feeling sorry for herself. She dramatically cried to her mother, "Will gets to do *everything* first! When will I ever get to do anything first?!" After some time of this lamenting, she finally noted with satisfaction, "At least he'll die first."

She managed to dwell contentedly on this fact for a few moments, but with a sudden realization she wailed, "But then he'll get to go to heaven first!" I can't help but wonder if the disciples in today's reading could relate even a little bit to my cousin's anguish.

READ ACTS 1:6-11.

Can you imagine what the disciples might have been thinking in Acts 1 when they saw their Lord, alive, go up to heaven "first," leaving them behind on earth with an important, specific mission? Perhaps they felt alone, and inferring from their question in verse 6, maybe a little confused, too: "Lord, are you restoring the kingdom to Israel at this time?"

This question was rooted in the popular idea that the Messiah would rule a political kingdom on earth to restore national sovereignty to Israel, freeing her from Roman rule.[3] Like the Samaritan woman we read about yesterday, Jesus' disciples had a set expectation for what the Messiah would do, and from what they could tell, Jesus' work on earth was not complete. But God had a different, better plan in mind, and that plan involved the power of the Holy Spirit and the birth and growth of the church.

READ JOHN 16:7. Why is it better that Christ went away?

Jesus said having the Holy Spirit is for our "benefit" (CSB) or "advantage" (ESV). Through the Holy Spirit, God is with us in every moment as our Helper. Write down a few specific ways the Holy Spirit has guided you in your Christian walk.

Like even my three-year-old cousin understood (to a degree), going to heaven through salvation is the greatest gift we can receive at the end of our lives on earth. There, we'll spend eternity in perfect communion with God, glorifying Him. That is the deferred hope for which our hearts long. We celebrate Christ's birth during Advent because through Him, God made that future possible. Every person who believes in Jesus has immediate access to God through the Spirit dwelling within him or her today, while simultaneously anticipating the final consummation of the kingdom of God. That's a big deal, and it comes with a big purpose. While we wait for Jesus to come back, we are called to be the church, His representation on earth. Jesus commanded that we, as the church, have some action steps to take now.

A favorite Christmas hymn of mine, "Go, Tell It on the Mountain," describes the joyful and action-oriented nature of this season of waiting we find ourselves in:

> Down in a lowly manger
> The humble Christ was born,
> And God sent us salvation
> That blessed Christmas morn.
>
> Go, tell it on the mountain,
> Over the hills and everywhere;
> Go, tell it on the mountain
> That Jesus Christ is born![4]

That is the gospel, the good news of salvation for all people in Jesus. Although He was a humble baby born in a lowly manger, Jesus' birth initiated a sequence of earthshaking events that made our salvation possible. These actions are what the Father called Him to do. God also calls us to action. He tells us to "Go."

MATTHEW 28:16-20 AND ACTS 1:8 GIVE US OUR MARCHING ORDERS. READ AND COMPARE THE TWO PASSAGES.

What's the mission of every Christian?

Jesus didn't mince words. The mission of His followers is to spread the good news about Him around the world. Despite the simplicity of these straightforward steps in our Great Commission, don't we, as believers, still catch ourselves becoming idle in our role, failing to prioritize the command to share the gospel or treat it with the urgency it deserves? Since our gift of salvation is free and can't be lost, human nature can cause us to become lazy and distracted. Jesus emphasized that disciple-making is the action all believers need to be taking today.

When God saves you, He seals you with the Holy Spirit (2 Cor. 1:22). Your salvation is secure in Him, and your commission is fueled by His power. You must seek to mature in your faith and disciple-making over time, but you have a testimony from your first moment as a believer. Once you're a child of God, you become a witness of His grace.

What is one change you can make to take a more action-oriented, Great Commission approach to this Advent season?

NOW, TURN TO ACTS 1:12-14. Who was present (that's mentioned), and what was their first course of action after the ascension?

Based on these verses we just read, it's apparent this time was uniquely challenging for believers. Unity through prayer was immediately necessary. In a time when Jesus' disciples may have felt alone as they waited for the Spirit's arrival, together they turned to God in prayer.

Dr. J. Vernon McGee notes, "There is no way that we can duplicate this period today. Remember that this is in a time period, a time capsule, between [Jesus'] ascension into heaven and the coming of the Holy Spirit. You and I do not live in that time period … We are not waiting for the coming of the Holy Spirit."[5]

As already noted this week, we live in a period of already but not yet, a time of deferred hope. With the Holy Spirit active in our lives, we can take part in God's kingdom here on earth. However, the kingdom will not reach its fullest expression until Jesus' return. Until then, God chooses to involve us, the church, in the urgent work that remains. How incredible that the plan of the omniscient God of the whole universe involves you and me!

When you're tempted to despair over the hardships in our world or the delay in Jesus' return, focus your eyes on the purpose you know God has given you for today. And if you feel unqualified in the actions Christ asks you to take, remember that when you seek first His kingdom and righteousness, you have nothing to be anxious about (Matt. 6:33). The Holy Spirit will be your Helper and Counselor regardless of your strengths or weaknesses. He intercedes for you as you pray and fills you with power to be a witness for our Lord.

> **Do you have a hard time remembering to stop before you speak, taking time to pray first? Or on the other hand, do you find yourself spending time praying about a loved one's salvation but failing to follow up and share the good news with him or her? Why are both important?**

> **What's a specific step you can take this week toward growth in your area of greater weakness?**

> **Close with a prayer of gratitude for the Spirit's working in your life, empowering you to serve as a witness for Him to the end of the earth. As you hopefully anticipate the future fulfillment of the kingdom, you can know that even in the waiting, you aren't alone.**

DAY 5

LOOK PAST THE PAIN

by Lynley Mandrell

"Sticks and stones may break my bones, but words will never hurt me." This childhood chant wrongly implies that hurtful words cannot cause pain and thus will be ignored or disregarded. Who came up with this? In my experience, words can be excruciating and cause far greater suffering than physical actions. When it comes to things in life that threaten our hope in Christ, which we've considered this week, the pain others cause us is certainly on that list.

Rejection is hard, and I've felt the sting many times throughout ministry. Several years ago, our family moved to Denver, Colorado, to begin a church in an area with very few churches. It was naturally unnerving to some of our neighbors who heard we had "come to convert them." Church planting wasn't a familiar concept, and they felt we were coming to judge them. When one feels uncertain, fear and self-protection can come into play, so we immediately saw the signs of tension on our new street.

The signs of unrest began in the form of fines from our homeowner's association (HOA) for having small gatherings at our house. As these citations continued, my husband appeared before the board to ask if they could provide clarity on these issues. He was told, "Sir, your neighbors are watching you and they don't like what they see. If I were you, I would consider moving to a different neighborhood." Neither he nor I could wrap our minds around how they were treating us.

The HOA wasn't the only group causing us heartache. One day in the street, a neighbor said, "The problem with your family is that you've moved in and made us all think about our worldview." While she did not personally have a problem with our church, she was speaking on behalf of a mysterious group that had decided we were up to no good.

> **Think about your own experiences with rejection. Why is being hurt by others so painful?**

What impact have those moments had on the way you approach relationships with other people? On the way you approach your relationship with God?

Our modern-day examples of rejection are painful, but they pale in comparison to what Peter and the apostles faced as they sought to spread the good news of God's love. In Acts 4, we read about the persecution experienced by the early church and the positive things that resulted from it. Perhaps you are going through a season of rejection and wondering if God sees you in your struggle. If so, take note of the hope that is ours in Christ when we learn to look past the pain of persecution.

> **READ ACTS 4:1-5.** **How did people respond to Peter and John as they shared the gospel?**

Remember, before Jesus ascended to heaven, He charged His disciples with spreading the good news about Him wherever they went. But the people in Peter and John's day quickly became "annoyed" by their message. In response, they did far more than report to the HOA. They "seized them and took them into custody" (v. 3). By today's standards, this was hardly a fruitful day in ministry. Yet, from God's perspective, the struggle was producing something beautiful: a newfound boldness from a faith that had been tested. The Bible states: "But many of those who heard the message believed, and the number of the men came to about five thousand" (v. 4).

Rejection creates boldness. Often, when we feel like the world is rejecting the message of Christ, He is doing His greatest work within us. As we realize the cost of our faith, the value rises along with our eagerness to share it. Later in the chapter, we read that those who rejected the apostles eventually took notice of their passion: "When they observed the boldness of Peter and John and realized that they were uneducated and untrained men, they were amazed and recognized that they had been with Jesus" (v. 13).

As church planters, our family experienced the struggle of being in the minority, but this enlarged our faith as well as our desire to represent Christ well. We learned that not all rejection leads to ruin.

In addition to boldness, Acts 4 also describes the powerful unity felt in the family of God as they faced the loneliness together and prayed through their fears:

What stands out to you from the disciples' prayer in verses 29-30?

The Holy Spirit unified these first Christians. The hostile culture caused them to band together and to pray together like never before. Church history shows that persecution draws Christians together, and God can use the rejection to build the community of faith.

Is this type of unity through hardship something you have experienced as part of a body of believers? How did hardship or struggle impact your spiritual growth?

READ ACTS 4:32-35.

A third and final result of rejection is the heightened ministry inside the family of God. Rejection creates a generous spirit. The way that Luke describes the generosity of the early church is heartwarming.

These Christians took joy in giving to one another, meeting needs, and growing their relationships. They used their resources to edify and encourage one another. Their unity in Christ led to a sacrificial and generous lifestyle, putting the needs of the body of believers ahead of their own.

One of the special components of starting a church is the sacrifice required of the launch team. When a group of people are united in heart and mission, they often give out of the goodness of their hearts. One person on our team would often purchase all the snacks and supplies for the weekly kids ministry activities, refusing to turn in receipts. "It's not my money; it's God's money," she would say. And she's right. All that we have is His, and giving toward the kingdom is the highest use of our resources.

This Christmas season, as you celebrate the original advent of Jesus and look forward to His return, be challenged by the early church's example. God's plan for His children is that we would grow close to believers and serve Him together as we wait for His return. We can take comfort knowing that any rejection or suffering we face in the process will be used by God to make His glory known.

As you read in Acts 4 about the early church's rejection by the culture around them, which aspect of their example—boldness, unity, or generosity—are you most challenged by today?

Write down next steps you can take this week to spread the good news boldly, pray with others, and share your gifts with those in need.

Spend extended time in prayer today, asking God to transform any pain or rejection you have felt recently into an opportunity to glorify Him and strengthen your relationships.

SKY LANTERN LAMENT

by Lauren Ervin

This world is filled with injustice and oppression. However, we know from the promises of Scripture that God will ultimately redeem these situations. The promise is true, but the hard part comes in trusting God's faithfulness and remembering that He alone is our refuge and salvation.

When you can't take another second of the news and find yourself discouraged by the world's injustice, practice lamenting to God rather than sharing discouraging complaints with others.

WHAT IS LAMENT?

Think of lament as the transition between pain and promise. It is expressing deep sorrow for the travails of a nation and as a group asking for God's blessing or intervention. Lament psalms make up a large portion of the Book of Psalms, and we can learn a lot about how to lament from these examples. Read Psalms 6; 42–43; and 130 for a few examples.

HOW DO YOU LAMENT?

1. Turn to God in prayer.

2. Bring your complaints before Him.

3. Ask boldly for answers to your prayers.

4. Choose to trust Him and praise Him, regardless of the circumstances causing your lament.[6]

ACTIVITY

Write a lament or prayer on a piece of flying wish paper or on a sky lantern. (You can find these online or at your local craft or hobby store.) Follow the instructions for how to light the lantern and release your lament.

PRACTICE LIVING GENEROUSLY

by Karen Daniel

Acts 1: 6 says, "Lord, are you restoring the kingdom to Israel at this time?" It's easy to see how the disciples would have expected Jesus to fix all the injustices in the world and restore His kingdom. After all, He was the Messiah, the long-awaited Savior who had come to deliver God's people. A normal question for a teenager to ask is why didn't God put an end to all the suffering while He was here physically on earth?

As you spend time with your teen this week, talk about some of the things you wish you could fix in the world. What injustices would you make right if you could? Have you ever considered why Jesus hasn't already corrected these problems?

READ ACTS 1:6-8.

It's not for us to know when Jesus will restore His kingdom, only to be His witnesses to the world. The Holy Spirit gives us the power to carry out this purpose. In the process, the church will grow and eventually reach the "ends of the earth" (v. 8). This is the in-between time, the already but not yet, a season of hope deferred we've read about this week. Jesus has come, but His kingdom hasn't yet been restored, and we deal with the pain points of that reality on a daily basis.

Teens often feel stuck in their own version of the already but not yet. They may already be able to drive, hold a job, and even lead organizations, yet they're not quite ready to live on their own or make their own financial decisions.

Jesus has invited all of us, including our teens, to participate in His plan to restore His kingdom. And He's always with us in the process.

With your teen, identify some injustices you actually can help fix this Christmas. Challenge your teen to contribute time and/or a financial gift, which really can make a difference in the world. Pick a project through your church, or partner with a Christian nonprofit organization at work in your community. Use the example of the early church from Acts 4 (Day 5's reading) as encouragement. Help your teen establish a lifelong habit of being Jesus' witness in the world through making a difference for others in His name.

MAKE A "STAINED GLASS" PICTURE

by Bekah Stoneking

Your home may be decorated and some wrapped presents may be starting to show up under the tree. It's already the Christmas season, but it's not yet Christmas Day. The already but not yet of Christmastime can feel frustrating, especially for our kids!

The Christmas season isn't the only in-between we are experiencing. The whole world is living in the middle of another, much bigger in-between season.

READ GALATIANS 4:4-7 AND ROMANS 5:6-8.

At the perfect time, God sent Jesus. Through Jesus' life, death, and resurrection, God's people get to participate in His kingdom now! We can worship and follow King Jesus, have forgiveness of sin, and enjoy fellowship with other believers.

But because of sin, there is sickness, pain, and sadness in our world. These things do not describe God's kingdom. Like we are waiting for Christmas, we are also waiting for God's kingdom to be on earth as it is in heaven.

While we wait, we can hope in God's power and control. The Book of Hebrews tells us that even when things seem bad, God is in control (Heb. 2:8). And the Book of Romans tells us that God works everything together for good (Rom. 8:28). This is what we need to always remember.

GATHER

- 2 square pieces of wax paper
- Black construction paper
- Scissors
- Glue stick
- Small pieces of colorful tissue paper

DIRECTIONS

Cut four thin strips of construction paper. Glue the strips around one square of wax paper like a frame. Then, think about one of your favorite promises from the Bible. Imagine how you would create a picture of that promise.

Rub glue all over the middle of the framed wax paper to make it sticky. Then, place the pieces of tissue paper on the sticky wax paper to create your picture. Cover the second square of wax paper with glue, and stick it on top of your picture to seal it.

Place your "stained glass" against a window or in your Christmas tree as a reminder that God always keeps His promises.

PRAY

God, on good days and bad days, You are in control. Help us to trust in You and to wait with hope as You fulfill Your promises. Amen.

the
light
of the
World

Jesus spoke to them again:
"I am the light of the world.
Anyone who follows me
will never walk in the
darkness but will have
the light of life."

JOHN 8:12

Hope in Tomorrow

THE KING'S RETURN

by Sarah Doss

Last week's study wasn't an easy one, as we discussed sin's effects in this world. Herod's slaughter of baby boys, the doubts of John the Baptist, and the tension the early church felt as they tried to follow Jesus' commands to share the good news of the gospel remind us that this world is still broken, and Jesus' work isn't finished. Thanks for sticking around; we know last week was tough.

But the good news is we're headed for brighter horizons in our final week of personal study together. That's how hope works, after all! This week, we'll unpack Jesus' teachings on how to live our lives in the here and now, while fixing our eyes on the then and forever in heaven.

Jesus didn't sugarcoat what it means to follow Him when He taught His disciples; in fact, He did the opposite. Jesus told them:

> You will have suffering in this world. Be courageous!
> I have conquered the world.
>
> John 16:33b

These words apply to us, too. In this world, we'll face hard things. Jesus promised that we would. But the message of Jesus and the message of the Advent season is, "Take heart" (v. 33, ESV). Even in the hard things, God is at work in you and in the world. He will sustain you, and He will keep His promises to you.

This week we're going to discuss the joy, redemption, and purpose that come from walking in step with Jesus day by day. We're going to unpack what it means that we have a living hope in Jesus and how that truth impacts our everyday lives.

We've been studying and praying over the stories of real people who responded to God's call with yeses of faith. We've talked about how their responsiveness to God's prompting led them on unconventional paths, but those paths brought great spiritual reward. Just for a moment, let's use "a Spirit-driven imagination, soaked in Scripture"[1] to put us into their sandals.

Can you fathom what it must have been like to be an unmarried young girl who was still a virgin and hear that you not only were going to have a child, but it would be the Son of God, the promised Messiah who would save the world? Can you imagine the great privilege of being face-to-face with the Son of God for years on end?

Or consider the life of Zerubbabel. What must it have been like to struggle and fight to restore the Davidic throne, to painstakingly lead efforts to restore God's temple—the place where He met with His children—and to remind people that God was at work, even as they were still recovering from the likely trauma of their exile in Babylon?

What about the magi? They followed a star and a prophecy to Bethlehem to meet the Messiah, and they found Him!

> God could have rescued the world in one fell swoop, but He didn't. He chose to use His children instead.

And of course we can't forget one of our first examples of faithfulness in Scripture—Abraham. God called him to leave behind his homeland and basically said, *I'll let you know when you've arrived where I want you to be, Abe, just keep that camel moving forward.* So, he did. Then he waited years and years to have a son whom God had promised him. And yet, Romans 4:20-21 gives us this report about Abraham: "He did not waver in unbelief at God's promise but was strengthened in his faith and gave glory to God, because he was fully convinced that what God had promised, he was also able to do."

As we head into this final week of personal study, I'm praying that God would make the same true in each of our hearts.

God, please make us stronger in our faith, help us to give You alone the glory for our lives and our work, and grant us the grace to walk each day fully convinced that You are able to do what You have promised to us. We want to be unwaveringly and joyfully confident in Your goodness to us today and always.

God chose each of these real people to play a part in His redemptive narrative—in the Advent of Jesus and the worship of the one true King. And since we are still waiting on His return, that means we have parts to play in the rest of the story.

This is the seemingly backward way of God's kingdom that we've talked about so many times before. God could've rescued the world in one fell swoop, but He didn't. He chose to use His children instead. He calls us to His work; He uses us to move forward the purposes of His kingdom; and as we say yes to God, we become part of His rescue mission, one that began in many ways with the coming of a tiny baby boy so many years ago. When we allow God to use us for His kingdom work, He changes us forever, in the best ways possible.

The coming of Jesus made a way for us to be with God forever. Those of us who trust in Jesus for salvation can say, "The incarnation means He became like us. The resurrection means we'll become like Him."[2]

But for now, we're still here, being sanctified day by day by the power of God's Word and the working of the Holy Spirit. While we wait for the joy of redemption to be completed, we share in the early church's work, the urgent call to tell others about Jesus and the hope of reconciliation to God available through belief in Him. God has given us a unique part to play in His redemptive narrative here on earth.

So what about you? How will you choose to participate in God's work here and around the world? Will you receive God's hope for you and follow His lead to brighter horizons? I hope and pray you will.

1 | If you're limited to just one choice, what do you have the hardest time waiting for in everyday life? What tests your patience the most?

2 | During Advent, we celebrate Jesus' birth and anticipate His return. When you think about the day when Jesus will come back, what most excites you? What are some other feelings that future hope stirs up for you?

3 | Read Matthew 28:16-20 and Acts 1:7-8. Jesus gave His followers (which includes His followers today) very clear marching orders. What are we to be doing while we wait for His return? When you evaluate your faithfulness to this task, what is your takeaway?

4 | The Christmas season is one of the few times of the year when Christianity continues to infiltrate the culture at large, giving you many opportunities to share the good news of the gospel with the people in your life. Who needs to hear from you about the love and salvation of Jesus? Come up with a plan as a group to hold each other accountable to living out the Great Commission this Christmas season.

5 | Close with some time in prayer. Thank God for the good news of the gospel message and your own salvation. Take turns praying by name for the people mentioned who need to know Jesus. Ask God for the strength and faithfulness to walk with Jesus daily while you wait for His return.

YOUR SORROW WILL TURN TO JOY

by Y Bonesteele

Sorrow. Sadness. Disappointment. These feelings usually come when life doesn't turn out the way we expect it to, the way we want it to. Whether we realize it or not, we have expectations and plans for what our lives should look like. Even as believers, we long for the "good life," however we define it, and we long for ease and comfort. So, when that doesn't happen for us, sorrow wells up. We wonder, *Why hasn't God provided?*

Perhaps instead of sorrow you feel a restlessness in your soul. You worry about political and racial tensions, poverty, the fate of the unborn. The news feeds remind you how broken our society is and you cry out: *Is this all there is, God?* Life rarely turns out the way we expect it to because God works beyond our expectations. In His knowledge, power, and creativity, He works out His plan, always for His ultimate glory and our ultimate good. But He asks us to trust Him while we wait and hope for it to play out. We can see this in the Christmas story, and we can see this in the Easter story. But for today, let's start backwards. Let's start with Easter.

READ JOHN 16:16-22.

While having their last meal together before His death, Jesus told the disciples,

> "In a little while, you will no longer see me; again in a little while, you will see me …" They said, "What is this he is saying, 'In a little while'? We don't know what he's talking about" (vv. 16-17).

Jesus' words to the disciples remind us how He continually tried to explain His mission and purpose to them; yet, until it happened, they were clueless about what was to come. Their cluelessness was a result of their expectations for the Messiah. They expected the Messiah to overthrow Roman rule. They expected Him to bring peace and end persecution of God's people. They expected deliverance. But Jesus had something else in store. He didn't want to overthrow Roman rule; He planned to overthrow Satan's rule. He wasn't there to bring peace between nations; He was there to bring peace to our souls. He wasn't going to deliver God's people from the authorities of the day; He was going to deliver God's people from sin, death, and shame, and do so with finality. So, Jesus confronted the disciples.

READ JOHN 16:20-22 AGAIN. What weeping, mourning, and sorrow was Jesus referring to?

What event would turn the disciples' sorrow into joy?

The disciples didn't understand what Jesus was about to do, but they soon would. Jesus foresaw the sorrow they would feel when He died, but He also told them of the joy to come when He would return to life.

You may be dealing with sorrow. Work can be laborious. Relationships can be difficult. Marriage can be mundane. Parenting can be exhausting. Finances can be strained. But through the hardship, through the struggle, pain, and sorrow, we have hope in a resurrected Christ who will return again and restore all things under His rule. Like the disciples, we have hope in a crucified Savior who rose again and who turns our sorrow into joy because He works beyond our expectations.

When have you found joy in something that initially was painful?

What do you find joy in today? Are your joys more often in temporary things or everlasting things?

Now let's backtrack to the Christmas story. Another story of sorrow turned to joy. A story of God going to great lengths because of His love for us.

READ PHILIPPIANS 2:7.

Jesus made many sacrifices on our behalf, the first of which was His incarnation. Jesus left behind the glory of heaven to become like us. We sometimes forget that the incarnation came with a cost. Jesus humbled Himself, separated Himself from the Father, and took on human limitations—a sacrifice we can't even begin to comprehend.

Mary, too, had to sacrifice in obedience to the Lord. The scandal of a pregnancy out of wedlock, a long journey into Bethlehem, giving birth in the stable of an inn. Surely, these events weren't how she imagined getting married and having her first child. Yet joy to the world was to come out of it.

Hope is found in the midst of sorrow and suffering. And when hope is found, peace is found. Jesus told His disciples in the Upper Room,

> I have told you these things so that in me you may have peace. You will have suffering in this world. Be courageous! I have conquered the world.

John 16:33

Let's not, then, be surprised when we suffer or experience sorrow. God isn't surprised. Jesus said we will have suffering. Expect trials; expect trouble. But, "count it all joy" (Jas. 1:2)! Through the sorrow, we will persevere and become more like Christ in His character.

"Be courageous!" Easier said than done sometimes, right? Courage is hard to muster up on our own. But with Christ by our side and the Spirit's power at work in us, we can stand up to fear. We can fight the battles ahead. We can trust in Jesus. Why? Because He has "conquered the world." Our hope isn't fickle; it isn't wishful thinking. Jesus has already done it. He's already victorious! Our hope is solid because Jesus is our solid rock. Our peace is secure because Jesus has secured victory through His resurrection. Our joy, then, is everlasting because Jesus is our everlasting hope fulfilled, and no one can take that away.

Let's remember that in Bethlehem, an empty manger waited for the Son of God to come to earth. Jesus was born in that stable, through pain and sorrow, against the expectations of those around Him. Years later, an empty tomb spoke into the world that God is victorious. Jesus, again, came to life, risen from the dead, victorious over all— again, through pain and sorrow, against the expectations of those around Him.

Jesus did all this for the glory of God and the good of us all, bringing about a joy beyond anything anyone expected. Christ cannot be bound by our expectations. He will do bigger and better things than we can imagine. He fills our emptiness with life. Joy to the world!

> Spend time today in reflection and prayer. Thank Jesus for His sacrifices in His incarnation and crucifixion. For emptying Himself to become human for us. For dying an excruciating death in a human body for us. Ask God to transform the difficulties in your life into moments of joy. Ask Him to help you find hope, even when things seem hopeless.

YOUR REDEMPTION IS DRAWING NEAR

by Kelly D. King

One of the fascinating trends of expectant parents these days is the popular gender reveal party. I have to admit I'm drawn to social media posts scattered with pink or blue balloons, confetti poppers, and cakes that spill over with candy announcing the gender of a coming baby. The joy of knowing a bit more about the little one who is coming lights up the faces of the parents, as well as the friends and family who surround them.

Most of us desire to know details about the future. We can learn from the past, experience the present, but the mystery of the future lives largely in our imaginations. This is why we like the glimpse of what is soon to come that we get from a gender reveal. We long for answers to big life questions, such as, *What kind of job will I have? Will I get married? Where will I live?* or *Will my children be successful?* Yet, God in His sovereignty asks each of us to trust Him with our future and to rest in the knowledge that He is working all things toward our good. Most of all, He wants us to hang on to the hope of His second coming.

What question about your future are you currently waiting on (and trusting in) God to answer?

Because humans are intrigued with the future, it's no surprise that Jesus addressed the subject of end times and His second coming during His earthly ministry. God promises to finish His work of redemption in our world, but the question of how is surrounded in mystery. So, Jesus pulled back the curtain a bit and gave not only His listeners but all of us a peek into the future.

For today's reading we will look mostly at Luke's Gospel, but all three of the Synoptic Gospels (Matthew, Mark, and Luke) include a section commonly known as the Olivet Discourse, which includes Jesus' teaching on the end times.

READ LUKE 21:25-28.

Once you've read the Luke 21 text, compare it with Matthew and Mark.

Compare the following passages and list similarities you find.

MATTHEW 24:29-31	MARK 13:24-27	LUKE 21:25-28

Think about the importance of road signs when you're driving. They serve to inform, warn, and can give you a glimpse of the road ahead. Paying attention to and obeying them is hugely important. The Old Testament prophets provided signs that pointed to the first coming of Jesus. By the time we get to Luke 21, Jesus Himself is the navigational system that reveals the signs of His second coming.

What signs are found in verses 25 and 26?

VERSE 25	
VERSE 26	

Think back to the story of Jesus' birth, recorded in Matthew 2. What was the cosmic sign of Jesus' first coming?

In Jesus' day, dramatic signs in the sky were more than occurrences for stargazers. As N. T. Wright explains, "People looked to the skies because they believed they would tell them about the imminent rise and fall of kings and empires. And when Jesus' disciples asked him how they would know when the frightening events he was talking about would take place, that's probably the sort of thing they had in mind."[3]

Do the signs in verses 25-26 cause you fear or anticipation? Think through why you answered that question the way you answered it.

If we stop at verse 26, the signs of the end of the world can seem quite scary. These are not the glimpses of our future we want to see. But hang on. Remember our study is about hope, and Jesus gives us exactly that in the next two verses.

READ LUKE 21:27. What's the hope of the end times? How did Jesus describe His own return?

The Greek word for power in this verse is *dynamis*, which means there is inherent power, power for performing miracles, moral power, and power that consists of force.

Look up the following verses and underline the word *power*:

Regarding Jesus' birth: Luke 1:35

Regarding Jesus' ministry: Luke 4:14

Regarding Jesus' followers: Acts 1:8

Not only did Jesus first come in power, but He lived with power, lives in us with power, and will also return with power! You and I can look forward to the second coming because Jesus is coming in power and glory. That's something to celebrate!

The second coming of Christ is a core doctrine of Christianity. Just as His first arrival is crucial for our faith, His return is also vital. Why? Because His second coming is the restoration of all things—creation and eternal redemption is coming for those who believe. New Testament believers encouraged each other in the midst of persecution with the hope of the second coming, and while the second coming didn't happen in their lifetimes, they hung on to the promise. We, too, still live in a broken and dying world that's full of fear and storms, but as followers of Jesus, we cling to the same promise of His return and the day when He will make all things right. Even if Jesus' return doesn't happen in our lifetime, we can still be confident that He will keep His promise. He's kept all the rest.

READ LUKE 21:28 AGAIN. **What did Jesus say we should do when these things take place?**

What's the great hope of verse 28?

How does this give you hope for your own future?

Just as Jesus' first arrival was right on time, His second coming won't be early or late. Hang on, sister. Jesus is coming!

YOU ARE NOT ALONE

by Debbie Dickerson

In my closet is a box filled with Christmas cards I've received over the years. During Advent, I display the glitter of hope and love sent from family and friends as we reconnect during the holidays, and then I add the cards to my collection. But three letters in unadorned envelopes always remain in the hallway beside my grandmother's picture. They represent the stacks of letters she sent me throughout the first years of my marriage. Those letters from home are filled with the richest stories of the most ordinary days. In tiny cursive writing penned in blue ink, they all start the same and end the same, and in-between are her prayers covering the day-to-day happenings at home—a neighbor in need, news from church, doctor appointments, grocery shopping, laundry day, life on the farm.

Her "ramblings," as she apologetically called them, created a treasure map I can trace down a long road rarely interrupted by postcard scenes. Each letter is a mile of life— letter by letter, mile by mile, much the same. But the riches lie between the lines that trail her history of hope: "I have faith in our dear Lord that He will do what I ask Him, if it's His will. Always remember to ask for His will to be done, for He has a plan and a purpose for our lives." Reading back over my grandmother's journey, I recognize the Holy Spirit as her constant companion guiding her with hope on her way home.

> **Whose life inspires you to walk daily with hope—perhaps someone from the lineage or life of Jesus or someone you know personally? How do you think that person lived purposefully during ordinary days?**

What difference did hope in God make in his or her story?

We all need hope because hope determines how we live. Looking at my Christmas cards, I see hope displayed in the "good news of great joy" (Luke 2:10). Since the fall of mankind, God promised to restore the relationship with His people that had been broken by sin. And just as He promised, "When the time came to completion, God sent his Son" (Gal. 4:4) as Immanuel in the manger, "God with us," the incarnate Jesus.

Think about it: Jesus took on flesh—fully God, fully man—to pay the penalty for our sin and secure our hope for eternal life with God. Jesus embodied that hope, living among mankind to show "the way, the truth, and the life" because "no one comes to the Father except through [Him]" (John 14:6). Even in His final hours of earthly life, as He walked toward the cross to rise out of the tomb, He left His disciples with a lasting lesson on living in hope.

READ JOHN 14:15-31. John 14 invites us to linger with Jesus after the last supper with His disciples. As you read verses 15–31, what words and phrases voice Jesus' desire for a relationship with us?

If you don't have a personal relationship with God, read "Becoming a Christian" on page 159, and ask God to show you how you may have eternal life in Him.

Because God is love, He desires a relationship with us. Throughout Scripture, He reminds us that He will never leave His children, and He reiterates that in verse 18. Jesus knew what awaited Him, and He knew that His followers would need hope to carry them until He came again to take them to His Father's house. (See John 14:1-3.)

In John 14:16, what did Jesus promise He would do?

During Old Testament days, the Spirit's role with the Father and Son was for specific tasks for selective individuals. In New Testament times, the Spirit existed fully in Jesus who was *with* the disciples to teach, lead, guide, and comfort them. But what would happen after Jesus returned to the Father's side? Jesus promised, "I will ask the Father, and he will give you another Counselor to be with you forever. He is the Spirit of truth" (vv. 16-17a).

Notice in verses 17 and 20 the words *with* and *in*. The Spirit wouldn't just be *with* them but would dwell *in* them—together forever with the Father, the Son, and the Spirit. What an amazing promise!

That was good news for the disciples, but it's also great news for any of us who confess Jesus is the Son of God. (See 1 John 4:15.) If you're a believer in Christ, then "you also were sealed with the promised Holy Spirit when you heard the word of truth, the gospel of your salvation, and when you believed. The Holy Spirit is the down payment of our inheritance" (Eph. 1:13-14a).

READ COLOSSIANS 1:27. If Christ is in you, what do you have?

I'm so thankful the Spirit isn't just a game-time cheerleader rallying us to keep our chin up through tough times. Instead, He lives in us continuously so that "the hope of glory" dwells in us. That is certain hope for today based on our eternal relationship with God. "Blessed be the Lord! Day after day he bears our burdens; God is our salvation" (Ps. 68:19).

So, how does the Spirit sustain our lives with hope? In John 14:26, Jesus said the Spirit would teach us God's truth and remind us of His words. "It is God who is working in you both to will and to work according to his good purpose" (Phil. 2:13). As we spend time in God's Word, the Spirit works in us to live in hope according to His purpose.

READ DEUTERONOMY 6:6-9. Locate the wonderfully practical plan God outlined for keeping His words in our hearts. We can put this into practice, trusting that the Spirit will teach and remind us of His truth.

1. In the morning when you're sitting quietly at home, select a truth from your Bible study that was meaningful to you. For example, for today's study, you might choose Colossians 1:27. Reflect on what the Spirit taught you from the context of the Scripture. Write the key verse on a note card as a visual reminder, and ask God to help you live by its truth throughout the day.

2. Keep the note card in view to reflect on the verse during routine tasks like washing the dishes or working at your computer. Voice the verse as a prayer, and ask God for guidance when you face challenges, deal with difficult relationships, or have opportunities to encourage family, friends, and coworkers.

3. Add to your nightly routine a time to thank God for specific ways the Holy Spirit has guided you.

Reminding ourselves of how the Spirit is with us throughout the day is like writing a letter to our heart. As we pen our own history of hope, we're saying, "I trust in you, LORD; I say, 'You are my God.' The course of my life is in your power" (Ps. 31:14-15a).

How do you want your living in the hope of glory to affect others who read your story?

DAY 4

YOUR WAIT IS WORTH IT

by Michelle R. Hicks

I have such sweet memories of my girls and their little eyes as they gazed longingly at the packages under the Christmas tree. Squeals of excitement would burst forth as the anticipation continued to build toward Christmas morning. The waiting was precious to observe as my girls looked forward to opening the surprises underneath the tree. But waiting isn't always so fun. To wait, for good or for bad, means to remain, to stand by, or hold back. It's a delay of action until something is ready.

> **Think about a recent season of waiting. What were you waiting for? What did you expect to happen? Circle or star the words that help describe your thoughts and feelings during that time.**

Aimless	Frustrated	Expectant
Anxious	Lingering	Restful
Content	Longing	Wasted time

We understand longing and waiting for Christ's return, and the Thessalonian believers understood it, too. In the early Christian church, the followers of Jesus began the wait for the Day of the Lord when He would return.

READ 1 THESSALONIANS 5:1-11.

Identify the words and phrases in 1 Thessalonians 5:1-11 that describe the Day of the Lord and jot them down. One phrase is listed to get you started.

Will come like a thief in the night

_____

_____

This waiting doesn't sound like the anticipation my girls experienced waiting to open their gifts. What the Thessalonians were waiting for sounds scary. The descriptions of the Day of the Lord and the second coming of Christ in 1 Thessalonians 5:1-11 are rooted in Old Testament prophecies. While the depictions may sound strange to our ears, they would've been well-known images for the Thessalonian believers.

Read the following verses and write down what you discover about the Day of the Lord from the Old Testament prophets.

ISAIAH 22:5; 13:9

JEREMIAH 30:7

JOEL 2:31

AMOS 5:18

ZEPHANIAH 1:14-16

MALACHI 4:1

It was natural for the new followers of Christ to identify the second coming of Jesus with the Day of the Lord. And it was natural for these believers to feel anxious wanting to know when that day would come. However, Jesus Himself had bluntly stated that no man knew when that day or hour would be, that even He did not know, that only God the Father knew. (See Matt. 24:26; Mark 13:32; and Acts 1:7.) God wants this day to be unexpected, but He wants His people to be prepared for the unexpected. As believers today, we don't need to experience anxiety or fear the future. We can live with great purpose and meaning in the days to come because we know Jesus and can trust Him.

READ MATTHEW 25:1-12, A PARABLE ABOUT BEING READY FOR JESUS' RETURN.

Think about a time when you prepared for the unexpected, such as a move, a new school, a job change, a baby, bad weather, a trip, or a new season of life. How did you prepare? What steps were you sure to take?

Now think about the parable from Matthew 25. In your own words, what does it look like to live ready for Jesus' return?

READ 1 THESSALONIANS 5:5-11 AGAIN.

In addressing the Thessalonians and their behavior, Paul simply told them to be who they were created to be in Christ. He wanted them to live up to what God had made them to be—people of light (v. 5). Our spiritual condition should reflect light and life in Christ, not darkness. Believers are to be spiritually active and aware, not asleep. We are to be sober and self-controlled, knowing the value of Christ and living in obedience to His ways. All of these behaviors and building of character prepare us to enter Jesus' presence. The timing of the Day of the Lord may be unexpected for the believer but that doesn't mean one has to be unprepared.

Describe the purpose of the spiritual armor Paul mentioned in 1 Thessalonians 5:8-11. How does each piece help us while we wait for Jesus' return?

SPIRITUAL ARMOR	ITS PURPOSE

Before we had the hope of salvation through Jesus, we had an appointment with the wrath of God. As believers we are saved from the world, the flesh, and Satan, but more importantly, we are rescued from the wrath of God that we deserve. Jesus has canceled our appointment by His substitution for us on the cross. His death was death, so that ours would only be sleep. Our Hope has come!

In the meantime, one of the ways we live with great purpose and meaning and prepare for the unexpected Day of the Lord when Christ returns is by building one another up, giving comfort and encouragement to others (v. 11).

READ 1 THESSALONIANS 5:23-24. Paraphrase this blessing in your own words or write out the verses.

Paul said "your whole spirit, soul, and body" will be "kept sound and blameless" on the Day of the Lord as Christ returns. Why is this good news? How does it strengthen your hope today?

Paul made it clear that sanctification is God's work in us. He is faithful. He will do it. It's by His strength and power that we can live with great purpose and meaning in the days to come. God sets us apart—spirit, soul, and body—the whole being is preserved by Him. This is how God works from the inside out. This is the blessing that echoes Colossians 1:27, "Christ in you, the hope of glory."

How will you live differently today remembering that Christ is at work in you and in our world and that He will finish that work when He returns on the Day of the Lord?

How will you live with greater purpose and meaning in the days to come?

YOUR HOPE IS ALIVE

by Elizabeth Hyndman

Peter has to be one of the most well-known and quite likely one of the most beloved people in the Bible. We admire his willingness to jump into the sea to walk on water (Matt. 14), his begging Jesus to please wash his head and his hands if that makes him clean (John 13), or his quickness with a sword to defend Jesus against the men arresting Him (John 18).

We might also see a bit of ourselves in Peter—reluctantly so—when he loses focus and falls into the water, when he still doesn't quite get why Jesus is serving him, and when he denies ever knowing the Messiah.

One of Peter's finest moments came when he received a commissioning on a beach over breakfast in John 21. After he had followed Jesus, denied Jesus, and watched Him die, Peter went back to what he knew. He fished. When the resurrected Jesus appeared to him, Peter jumped right into the water to swim to His Savior on the shore (John 21:7). We should expect nothing less from Peter!

Jesus told Peter to feed His sheep, to shepherd them. He told him three times. It is this Peter, the shepherd, who wrote 1 Peter to the church scattered abroad. Most scholars think this first letter from Peter was written during the time of Nero, when persecution of Christians started to accelerate across the Roman empire. We can assume the recipients of this letter were tired. They had suffered, they were suffering, and there wasn't a clear end in sight. They needed hope.

READ 1 PETER 1.

What do you learn about the recipients of this letter, based on the first two verses?

The letter starts with "To those chosen." Peter wrote to believers. He wrote to those who were being sanctified through the Holy Spirit, who were trying to be obedient, and who had been "sprinkled with the blood of Jesus Christ" (1 Pet. 1:2).

The next section (vv. 3-9) is powerful. Read it again, this time out loud if you're in a place where you can.

> **According to verses 3-4, what is it that we are given? On whose merit do we receive such a gift?**

> **What word describes the hope we're born into?**

The word used to describe hope in the original Greek language is *zaō*. It's translated as "living" in many Bible translations (v. 3, CSB, ESV, NASB, NIV). One Greek dictionary describes the word this way, in the context of 1 Peter 1:3, "having vital power in itself and exerting the same upon the soul."[4] As you've been reading throughout this entire study, hope is a powerful thing. And this hope? This is real, living hope.

> **What do you think it means to have a "living" hope?**

> **Read verse 6 again. What are we to do, even in the midst of suffering?**

Verse 6 brings us back to reality with the reminder that this world is wrought with trials. Only those who have a living hope, a hope they are born into through Christ's mercy, can rejoice in the midst of suffering. Later on in this same letter, Peter told the church to be "ready at any time to give a defense to anyone who asks you for a reason for the hope that is in you" (1 Pet. 3:15). If we're rejoicing with an "inexpressible and glorious joy" (1 Pet. 1:8), even when we're going through trials, then people are going to ask about that. And we get to tell them about our living Hope and how they, too, can be born into it.

Look now at verses 10-12. Rewrite this paragraph in your own words.

This paragraph perfectly sums up our entire Advent study! The prophets got to see only glimpses of the gospel in the things they foretold. They knew the coming Messiah would suffer (Isa. 53), and they wanted to know when all these things would pass. Although that information was never theirs to know, they maintained their hope in God's promises and did their part to fulfill His plans.

On the other side of the Old Testament, we know the answer to the "When?" question for the first advent of Christ, but we're still waiting on the "When?" of the second. We know God fulfills His promises because of the testimony of the prophets and the people of the Bible. We look forward—with hope—to the fulfillment of the rest, the eternal inheritance (life with God forever and the new heaven and earth!) Peter mentioned in verse 4.

Now look at verses 13-25. What are we supposed to do in light of our rebirth into a living hope? List the specific commands.

-
-
-
-
-
-

Did any of the commands surprise you? Which ones are hardest for you to live out?

If you think back to English class, you may remember learning about imperatives and indicatives. Indicatives indicate something is true; they state a fact. Imperatives, on the other hand, are commands. ("It is imperative that you do this!") Often in Scripture we'll see indicatives first. We learn what is true about Christ and ourselves in light of who Christ is. Then, the writer will bring in imperatives. Because of what we learned about who Christ is, therefore, we must do a, b, and c.

I love this paragraph in 1 Peter 1 because it mixes them all in together. In true Peter-jumping-right-in fashion, it's as if he was so excited about who Jesus is and what He's done for us that Peter couldn't help inserting it into every sentence.

What indicatives can you find in this paragraph? Or, stated another way, what does this passage teach you about Christ?

How does that change the way you think about the imperatives or the commands you listed earlier?

While we wait for Jesus' return, our living Hope motivates us to pursue holy living. Like the example of the persecuted Christians who were able to rejoice through suffering, the way we live in the meantime will catch the attention of others. This is just one of the many ways God continues to use this time to draw people to Himself.

As we close out this study and turn toward a new season and a new year, we can have hope, no matter what the world around us looks like. Because of Jesus, our hope is alive. Our hope looks forward to a future that is promised and sealed, an inheritance that is "imperishable, undefiled, and unfading, kept in heaven for you" (1 Pet. 1:4).

We, too, can rejoice with "inexpressible and glorious joy" (v. 8) because our faith and hope—the living, powerful Hope—are in God (v. 21). That hope is sure.

NOTES

ENCOURAGEMENT ORNAMENTS

by Lauren Ervin

In the midst of endless chores, difficult relationships, and unexpected challenges daily life throws at us, we could all use words of genuine encouragement. Even a short note of thankfulness goes a long way. Use this activity to make a small token for those who you want to encourage. If the note is short, write it on the back of the ornament in permanent marker. Otherwise, hang an index card or small notepaper with it. Consider hanging the ornament on the recipient's front door or taping it to a small gift.

RECIPE

This recipe uses cornstarch and baking soda to create a smooth, white, clay-like dough that will air dry.

Cook time: 10 minutes

INGREDIENTS

- 2 cups baking soda
- 1 cup cornstarch
- 1 1/4 cup cool water

SUPPLIES

- A glass bowl
- Cookie stamps or cut greenery
- Cutters
- A drinking straw

DIRECTIONS

Combine baking soda and cornstarch in a medium saucepan. Stir in cool water and mix completely. Set pan over medium heat and stir constantly. At about 5–7 minutes, mixture will begin to turn slightly golden or toasted, then it will begin to bubble. Continue stirring for another 2–3 minutes as it thickens and comes together. Transfer to a glass bowl. Cover with a damp cloth. Let mixture cool for at least one hour.

Knead cooled dough until smooth. Roll out to desired thickness, using more cornstarch if needed to keep it from sticking. Stamp or press rolled dough using cookie stamps or found items like cut greenery. Cut with cutters, and use a drinking straw to punch out a hole for hanging.

Let ornaments dry for 24 hours.

EXTRA IDEA

Write an encouraging note along with the year on the back. Tie it to your gifts as a finishing touch.

LIVE IN THE LIGHT

by Karen Daniel

"So then, let us not sleep, like the rest, but let us stay awake and be self-controlled" (1 Thess. 5:6).

If your teen is a member of a sports team or engaged in school clubs or projects, take some time this week to talk with him or her about the importance of being an active participant and what that looks like. If other teammates don't do their part, how does the whole team suffer? Why is it important to cheer each other on, not just in games but even in practice?

Spend some time in 1 Thessalonians 5:1-11 this week, and help your teen connect this passage with the importance of being an active participant in the body of Christ. In the same way it's important to show up, do our part, and encourage our teammates and fellow club members, we live with even greater purpose and meaning when it comes to our participation in God's kingdom.

As you talk about verse 6, don't lose hope. Most teens get a bad rap when it comes to how much they like to sleep. (Really, I think the rest of us are just jealous!) It's important for adults to recognize that teens are just as integral to God's plan as we are, or even as our pastors and other spiritual leaders are. They don't have to

wait to grow up to be used by God. Let's encourage them by example to stay awake (spiritually) and point others to Christ. Even though we "belong to the day," we still live in a world of darkness. In the same way it's important to encourage our teammates, it's important to encourage other believers and point others to Christ.

Issue a challenge to your teen this week to stay awake with you (this time, literally) 30 minutes more each day for seven days. Challenge your teen and yourself to either wake up early or stay up later each evening, spending that time in God's Word and praying for friends who need encouragement and who need to know Christ. Use the seven-day Scripture reading plan below as a guide for your time.

Living in the light means being in relationship with Christ every day. What better time to establish this lifestyle than during Advent. As children of the light, we don't have to worry about being unprepared when the Day of the Lord comes. Let's do what we can to be sure those we care about are prepared, too.

7-DAY SCRIPTURE READING

Go to lifeway.com/hope to find the 7-Day Scripture Reading Plan.

MAKE SOMETHING NEW

by Bekah Stoneking

God revealed His plans through Scripture, and He has already fulfilled some plans through Jesus.

God created everything and rules over it. People have chosen to break God's rules and sinned. The price of sin is death.

But God had a plan. God sent Jesus to live a perfect, sinless life; die on the cross; and rise again on the third day.

Jesus' death and resurrection did something we could never do for ourselves—He paid the price for our sin! Jesus alone offers us forgiveness of sin and adoption into God's family.

But that's not all! What do we have to look forward to that God hasn't done yet? God is working to make all things new. One day, Jesus will return, and we will be with God forever in the new creation—a place where there will be no more sin, pain, sickness, or sadness.

Locate and read the following verses:

- ISAIAH 43:18-19
- 2 CORINTHIANS 5:17
- REVELATION 21:1-3

These verses are all about how God is making everything new. Our hope in Jesus means we can have hope that new, good things are coming in His kingdom. And like every other part of God's plan, this new creation will come at exactly the right time.

ACTIVITY

Do you have a broken toy? Cardboard tubes or empty boxes in your recycling bin? Some torn clothing? Gather items like these and your favorite craft supplies. Work in partners or as individuals to have a competition turning your trash into treasures.

Describe your new creations to one another. Share pictures on a parent's social media. Write a post or make a video about the new creation you're looking forward to because of Jesus.

PRAY

Thank You, Jesus, for coming at the perfect time, living a perfect, sinless life, and dying on the cross to pay for our sins. Please help our family and friends turn away from sin and put our hope in You as Lord and Savior. Amen.

The
Word
became
flesh

The Word became flesh
and dwelt among us.
We observed his glory,
the glory as the one and
only Son from the Father,
full of grace and truth.
JOHN 1:14

Hope for Today

WEEK

FIVE

THE LORD'S FAITHFULNESS

by Sarah Doss

I don't know about you, but after Christmas each year I feel a little blue when the décor comes down and the sound of Christmas carols fades into the background. The beauty and wonder of the season bring me such joy. And I find that when I practice intentional waiting during the Advent season, I cherish the celebration and gift of the coming of Christ that much more. At Christmas, we praise God for being a faithful promise keeper. We celebrate His love for us and grace toward us—precious gifts, neither of which we did anything to earn.

I love how Pastor Scotty Smith puts it: "Advent says, 'Wait with hope.' Christmas says, 'Celebrate with joy.' The gospel says, 'I guarantee both.'"[1]

So even after the tinsel has lost its shine and the Advent wreath has been taken down, the gospel guarantee holds great promise for the rest of the year. I can celebrate God's faithfulness and be sustained by His character because His gospel grace sustains my hope.

You may be familiar with Proverbs 31. It's often cited as the model for what a godly woman should look like. In thinking about embracing our living Hope in the days to come, I'm particularly struck by Proverbs 31:25, which reads, "Strength and dignity are her clothing, and she laughs at the time to come." The Message paraphrase writes the second half of the verse as "… she always faces tomorrow with a smile."

Think back to Week Two of our study when we discussed the details of John the Baptist's birth narrative. Remember, Elizabeth and Zechariah, genuine followers of God who hadn't been able to have a child, were told that they would miraculously bear a baby boy in their old age. Elizabeth and Mary, Jesus' mom, were relatives. Soon after both Mary and Elizabeth were told they would have out-of-the ordinary birth stories, Mary visited Elizabeth. (You can review the full passage in Luke 1:39-45.)

At this visit, under inspiration of the Holy Spirit, Elizabeth said to Mary, "And blessed is she who believed that the Lord would fulfill what he has spoken to her!" (Luke 1:45).

And that's the note I want us to end our study on—one of hope and faith-filled praise to our God, one of greeting every sunrise with a knowing grin and believing that the Lord will fulfill what He has spoken to us.

Hebrews 11:6a says, "Now without faith it is impossible to please God." This means that faith is pleasing to God. And the testimonies of Proverbs 31:25 and Luke 1:45 show us that faith looks like taking God at His Word, living our lives in confident trust and rest, praising Him while we wait for the rest of His promise keeping.

As we strive to be women who have their gospel hopes up, who joyfully expect God to keep His promises and trust that He has good planned for us, and who can "face tomorrow with a smile," may God grow our trust in His tender care for us and His gracious hand in each and every one of our tomorrows.

As we close out our time together, let's finish by reading from Romans:

> Now may the God of hope fill you with all joy and peace as you believe so that you may overflow with hope by the power of the Holy Spirit.
>
> Romans 15:13

Commenting on Romans 15:13, the ESV Study Bible says, "Joy and peace come from trust in God, but such trust is finally the gift of God, for believers abound in hope only by his grace."[2]

I love that Paul used the phrase "the God of hope" to describe God in this passage. In the end, hope in God's character doesn't disappoint us because God doesn't just sustain our hope with His grace, He's the God of *all* hope. He's the Author of hope, and He's filling up our hearts and minds and world with it as He continues to redeem everything.

God holds hope for you in the days to come. Let's begin this new year with hearts full of joy, peace in believing, gratitude for God's presence with us both today and forever, and praise for His kindness to us.

Father, with hope-filled hearts, we look to You, the God of all hope. Please use us for Your glory.

1 Share one word that best describes how this Christmas season has been for you.

2 During our first group meeting, we wrote down our own definitions of *hope*. Look back at the definition you came up with on page 14. Would you make any changes to it now that we've arrived at the end of this Advent study and season of reflecting on the hope of Christ?

3 Read Proverbs 31:25 together. Does this verse describe you? What are some specific ways we can encourage each other (or verses we can repeat to ourselves) to trust God enough to laugh "at the time to come," to face tomorrow with a smile?

4 Think back over all of the people from Scripture you read about this month and the ways their hope in God and His promises impacted their lives. Whose example has stuck with you? What did you learn from that person's story that you are applying to your own relationship with God?

5 For your closing prayer time today, invite your group to take turns voicing prayers of gratitude and praise to God for sending Jesus, our great Hope. Pray that you would be women whose lives are marked by the joy and peace that come with placing your hope in Jesus every day. Pray for eyes fixed on the promise of Jesus' return, the day when our faith and hope give way to sight.

NOTES

CONTRIBUTORS

JOY ALLMOND

Joy Allmond serves as executive communications manager for Lifeway. She and her husband, Greg, are community group leaders in their local church (Grace Community Church, Brentwood, Tennessee) and have two sons.

TINA BOESCH

Tina Boesch serves as manager of the Lifeway Women Bible Studies team. She earned a Master of Arts in Theology at Regent College in Vancouver, British Columbia. For fourteen years, she and her husband and their three kids called Istanbul, Turkey, home. Now they've settled north of Nashville, but she still misses the view over the Golden Horn at sunset, steaming cups of Turkish tea, and walks along the Bosphorus Strait. Tina is the author of *Given: The Forgotten Meaning and Practice of Blessing*.

Y BONESTEELE

Y Bonesteele has her Master of Divinity from Talbot School of Theology and has lived on mission in Spain with her husband and four kids, but currently she resides in Middle Tennessee. During the Christmas season, she enjoys carrying on the Spanish tradition of creating an elaborate Nativity town, the *belen*, as it depicts all the busyness of Bethlehem on that night when God came near.

KAREN DANIEL

Karen Daniel serves as a publishing team leader for Lifeway Student Ministry. She's recently arrived on the other side of the teen parenting years and enjoys sharing what she learned along the journey with anyone interested to listen. She also starts every day with a Wonder Woman® coffee mug and the joy of knowing that the God of the universe always has her back.

DEBBIE DICKERSON

Debbie Dickerson and her husband, Steve, love spending time with their oldest son, Landon, and his wife, Alyssa, and their college-aged son, Kaden. Debbie enjoys serving as editor of *Mature Living* and as a children's teacher at ClearView Baptist Church in Franklin, Tennessee.

SARAH DOSS

Sarah Doss is the team leader for the Lifeway Women Bible Studies team. With an educational background in communications from the University of Georgia, this Georgia peach now calls Nashville, Tennessee, home. In her spare time, Sarah enjoys watching quirky sitcoms, a strong cup of coffee, and travel (international or otherwise).

CONTRIBUTORS

LAUREN ERVIN

Lauren Ervin is a graphic designer on the Lifeway Women Bible Studies team. She is an avid photographer, doodler, and chart maker. In her downtime, she chases around her two adorable toddlers with the help of her husband and dog.

ERIN FRANKLIN

Erin Franklin is a production editor on the Lifeway Women Bible Studies team. A graduate of Lipscomb University, she enjoys a good ping-pong match, photography, and learning new things. You can connect with her on Instagram @erin_franklin and on Twitter @erinefranklin.

ASHLEY MARIVITTORI GORMAN

Ashley Marivittori Gorman (MDiv) serves as an associate publisher at B&H Publishing Group, an imprint of Lifeway Christian Resources. She has been trained under The Charles Simeon Trust, and her passions are biblical literacy, discipleship, theology, foster care, and books. Ashley and her husband, Cole, live in Nashville with their daughter, Charlie.

MICHELLE R. HICKS

Michelle R. Hicks is the managing editor for *Journey* devotional magazine with Lifeway Women. Michelle served as a freelance writer, campus minister, and corporate chaplain before coming to Lifeway. She is a graduate of the University of North Texas and Southwestern Baptist Theological Seminary, and is currently pursuing a doctoral degree at Gateway Seminary. Michelle has a deep hunger for Scripture and desires to help women grow in their faith and understanding of God's Word. Connect with her @michellerhicks.

SUSAN HILL

Susan Hill is a writer, Bible teacher, and full-time editor at Lifeway. She is the author of *Dangerous Prayer: 50 Powerful Prayers That Changed the World*, as well as numerous devotional books. She and her husband, John, live near Nashville, Tennessee, with two unruly Goldendoodles. You can read her blog at susanhillblogs.com.

ELIZABETH HYNDMAN

Elizabeth Hyndman writes, edits, and tweets. Officially, she's a social media strategist at Lifeway where she uses both her English undergraduate and her seminary graduate degrees every day. Elizabeth grew up in Nashville, sips chai lattes every chance she can get, and believes everyone should have a "funny picture" pose at the ready. Follow her on Twitter or Instagram at @edhyndman.

CONTRIBUTORS

KELLY D. KING

Kelly D. King is the manager of magazines/devotional publishing and women's ministry training for Lifeway Christian Resources and the cohost of Lifeway Women's *Marked* podcast. She is the author of *Ministry to Women: The Essential Guide for Leading Women in the Local Church*. Kelly has a Master of Theological Studies degree from Gateway Seminary and is currently pursuing her Doctorate of Ministry degree. She loves living in the Nashville area but is forever an Oklahoman at heart.

LYNLEY MANDRELL

Lynley Mandrell is the wife of Ben Mandrell, the president and CEO of Lifeway. Before coming to Lifeway, Ben and Lynley spent five years in Denver, Colorado, planting a church designed to reach the unchurched. She is a mother of four and a fan of Reese's Peanut Butter Cups®, Dr. Pepper®, and silence.

RAVIN MCKELVY

Ravin McKelvy is a copywriter at Lifeway and graduated with a degree in communications from Moody Bible Institute. She is passionate about the intersection of art and theology and sharing the daily realities of Christian living on Instagram. Ravin grew up in a family of twelve, and she currently lives with some of her family in Franklin, Tennessee.

TESSA MORRELL

Tessa Morrell is a production editor for ongoing curriculum at Lifeway. An Illinois native, Nashville, has become her home of more than ten years. She is passionate about serving in her local church and studying the Word of God with others in Bible study. When she's not busy reading, she enjoys visiting local coffee shops, spending hours browsing in antique stores, and crafting and creating art.

CONNIA NELSON

Connia Nelson is the senior vice president & CHRO for Lifeway. She is passionate about the ministry of the local church and is currently an active part of Rolling Hills Community Church. Connia earned her Master of Arts in Organizational Management from Dallas Baptist University in Dallas, Texas. She and her husband, Darrell, have one married daughter, and she is proud to be "CeCe" to her two precious grandsons.

CAROL PIPES

Carol Pipes is director of corporate communications at Lifeway. She's an avid reader, a morning coffee drinker, and is known to randomly and unexpectedly break out in song. She and her husband, Keith, live in Nashville. Follow her on Twitter @CarolPipes.

CONTRIBUTORS

YVONNE FAITH RUSSELL

Yvonne Faith Russell is a passionate writer, editor, dancer, teacher, and choreographer. A Nashville native, she manages two careers in publishing and performing arts. Yvonne is the author of *A Word to the Wise: Lessons I Learned at 22*, a book dedicated to helping young women conquer life after graduation. Yvonne also serves as a production editor for Lifeway Christian Resources.

RACHEL SHAVER

Rachel Shaver works with books at Lifeway by day, and by night, wrangles three sweet, rowdy kids. She affectionately refers to them as the "mafia." Rachel and her husband, Evan, make their home in a little town right outside of Nashville, Tennessee.

AMANDA MAE STEELE

Amanda Mae Steele is a writer, photographer, and performing artist based in Franklin, Tennessee. She lives with her husband, Nick, baby girl, and twelve-year-old "puppy," Dino. Amanda Mae is passionate about God's Word, traveling, people, and music. She serves as the B&H Kids Marketing Specialist at Lifeway.

BEKAH STONEKING

Bekah Stoneking serves as the research specialist and content editor for Explore the Bible: Kids at Lifeway. With experience as a children's minister and elementary school teacher, Bekah is passionate about teaching, learning, making disciples, and equipping others to do the same. She is currently completing her doctoral dissertation at SEBTS. Bekah lives in Nashville, Tennessee, where she is a member and a children's Sunday school teacher at The Church at Avenue South.

MARY WILEY

Mary Wiley is the author of *Everyday Theology*. She holds a Master of Arts in Theological Studies and is passionate about helping women understand and live God's Word. She and her family live in Lebanon, Tennessee, where they attend and serve at Fairview Church. Mary leads the marketing team at B&H Publishing Group and loves words, books, paper, and coffee. Connect @marycwiley.

JESSICA YENTZER

Jessica Yentzer is a marketing strategist for Lifeway Women. Well-written memoirs, dark chocolate, a good running trail, and the perfect fall day are just a few of the things that put a smile on her face. When she's not planning marketing strategy, she loves hiking and exploring the outdoors with her husband, Grant.

THE ADVENT WREATH

Few seasons in life come with as many traditions as Christmas. From the trees to the stockings, to the feasting, music, and Christmas movies on repeat, this time of year is marked by things that bring us joy and fill us with memories. We can all agree, though, that the traditions that mean the most are the ones that point us back to Jesus.

One popular tradition in many Christian homes and churches is the Advent wreath. Advent wreaths vary, especially around the world, but most common is a wreath made of evergreen garland (which symbolizes eternal life) that holds five candles: three purple, one pink, and one white. The purple candles symbolize hope, love, and peace; the pink candle symbolizes joy; and the white candle symbolizes Christ. Each candle is lit on one of the Sundays of Advent, with the Christ candle being lit on Christmas Eve or Christmas Day.

Whether an Advent wreath is a new concept for you or a longstanding tradition in your family, we invite you to join us on this journey this Advent. You can use the Scripture passages and prayers below to guide you through the weeks as you make this tradition your own. (And by all means, use whatever color candles you have!)

ADVENT WREATH SCHEDULE

FIRST SUNDAY OF ADVENT

Theme: Hope
Candle: Purple
Scripture: Isaiah 9:2
Prayer: Prayerfully consider the hope God brings to the world through Jesus, and the hope we have in His promised return.

SECOND SUNDAY OF ADVENT

Theme: Peace
Candle: Purple
Scripture: Isaiah 9:6-7
Prayer: Prayerfully consider God's peace coming into our hearts and minds and the peace Jesus brings between us and God. Pray also for the peace our world desperately needs, peace only possible through belief in Jesus and the reconciliation He brings.

THIRD SUNDAY OF ADVENT

Theme: Joy
Candle: Pink
Scripture: Matthew 2:10-11
Prayer: Prayerfully consider the incomparable joy that we can know in God alone.

FOURTH SUNDAY OF ADVENT

Theme: Love
Candle: Purple
Scripture: John 3:16-17
Prayer: Prayerfully consider God's unconditional love for us and our call to reflect the love of Christ to others.

CHRISTMAS EVE/DAY

Theme: Jesus
Candle: White
Scripture: John 8:12
Prayer: Prayerfully consider the light Jesus brought into a dark and desperate world at His incarnation, and the light He continues to shine in our world today. Pray for the courage and faith to be a light in the world who shines for Him (Matt. 5:14).

ADDITIONAL READINGS

Isaiah 9:2-7
Matthew 1:18–2:12
Luke 2:1-20
John 1:1-18
Galatians 4:4-7
Philippians 2:5-11

ENDNOTES

WEEK 1

1. "Hope," Oxford Lexico Online. Available at www.lexico.com/en/definition/hope.

2. "Kevin McAllister," *Home Alone,* Hughes Entertainment, 1990.

3. See "Genesis 49:10," https://biblehub.com/commentaries/genesis/49-10.htm for various scholars who support "he whose right it is" refers to Jesus.

WEEK 2

1. Zack Eswine, *Spurgeon's Sorrows: Realistic Hope for those who Suffer from Depression* (Christian Focus, 2015).

2. Max Anders and Trent C. Butler, "Luke 2—The Savior's Earthly Birth and Heavenly Mission," *Holman New Testament Commentary, Vol. 03: Luke* (Nashville, TN: B&H Publishing Group, 2012).

3. Dr. David Jeremiah, Notes on verse 32, *The Jeremiah Study Bible, ESV: What It Says. What It Means. What It Means for You* (Worthy, 2019).

4. Kristi McLelland, *Jesus and Women: The First Century and Now* (Nashville, TN: Lifeway, 2020).

WEEK 3

1. J. I. Packer, as quoted in Matt Smethurst, "40 Quotes from J. I. Packer (1926–2020)" July 17, 2020. Available online at thegospelcoalition.org.

2. David Platt, *Christ-Centered Exposition: Exalting Jesus in Matthew* (B&H Publishing Group, 2013), 145-148.

3. "Note on Acts 1:6," ESV Study Bible (Wheaton, IL: Crossway, 2008).

4. John W. Work, Jr., "Go, Tell It on the Mountain," *Baptist Hymnal* (Convention Press, 1991), 95,

5. J. Vernon McGee, *Thru the Bible: Matthew–Romans, Vol. 4* (Nashville, TN: Thomas Nelson, 1983), 513.

6. Mark Vroegop, "Dare to Hope in God: How to Lament Well," Desiring God. April 6, 2019. Available online at www.desiringgod.org.

WEEK 4

1. Gloria Furman, Noteworthy Quotes on "The Global Church with Gloria Furman," Journeywomen Podcast. Available at https://journeywomenpodcast.com/episode/global-church.

2. Attributed to Dan DeWitt, as quoted by @MattSmethurst, Twitter, Dec. 22, 2020.

3. N. T. Wright, *Luke for Everyone, Society for Promoting Christian Knowledge* (London, 2004). https://app.logos.com/books/LLS%3AEVRY63LU/references/bible.63.21.5-63.21.19.

4. "*Zao,*" *Thayer's Greek Lexicon,* Electronic Database. Copyright © 2002, 2003, 2006, 2011 by Biblesoft, Inc. All rights reserved. Used by permission. BibleSoft.com Accessed via blueletterbible.org, 3 December 2020.

WEEK 5

1. Scotty Smith, Emeritus Christ Community, Twitter, @ScottyWardSmith, Dec 3, 2020.

2. "Note on Romans 15:13," ESV Study Bible (Wheaton, IL: Crossway, 2008).

BECOMING A CHRISTIAN

Romans 10:17 says, "So faith comes from what is heard, and what is heard comes through the message about Christ."

Maybe you've stumbled across new information in this study. Or maybe you've attended church all your life, but something you read here struck you differently than it ever has before. If you have never accepted Christ but would like to, read on to discover how you can become a Christian.

Your heart tends to run from God and rebel against Him. The Bible calls this sin. Romans 3:23 says, "For all have sinned and fall short of the glory of God."

Yet God loves you and wants to save you from sin, to offer you a new life of hope. John 10:10b says, "I have come so that they may have life and have it in abundance."

To give you this gift of salvation, God made a way through His Son, Jesus Christ. Romans 5:8 says, "But God proves his own love for us in that while we were still sinners, Christ died for us."

You receive this gift by faith alone. Ephesians 2:8-9 says, "For you are saved by grace through faith, and this not from yourselves; it is God's gift—not from works, so that no one can boast."

Faith is a decision of your heart demonstrated by the actions of your life. Romans 10:9 says, "If you confess with your mouth, 'Jesus is Lord,' and believe in your heart that God raised him from the dead, you will be saved."

If you trust that Jesus died for your sins and want to receive new life through Him, pray a prayer similar to the following to express your repentance and faith in Him:

Dear God, I know I am a sinner. I believe Jesus died to forgive me of my sins. I accept Your offer of eternal life. Thank You for forgiving me of all my sins. Thank You for my new life. From this day forward, I will choose to follow You.

If you have trusted Jesus for salvation, please share your decision with your group leader or another Christian friend. If you are not already attending church, find one in which you can worship and grow in your faith. Following Christ's example, ask to be baptized as a public expression of your faith.

Get the most from your study.

Customize your Bible study time with a guided experience.

In this 5-session Advent study, you'll find encouragement from the lives of people in the Bible who trusted God's promises and said yes to God's plans. Join us as we celebrate God's kindness and choose to trust in His promises, even when the future seems uncertain. Yes, our Hope has come, and at just the right time, He will be back.

In this study you'll:

- Unpack the Christmas story and more to capture the wonder of the holiday season.

- Learn how to anchor your hope in the person and work of Jesus.

- Remember how God works on behalf of His children at just the right time.

ADDITIONAL RESOURCES

Visit **lifeway.com/hope** to explore both the Bible study book and eBook along with a free session sample and church promotional materials.

Want to share this book with a friend? It's also available for purchase on the **Lifeway Women app.**